T0065493

FAMILY MATTER
FATHER MOTHER SON DAUGHTER

DR. GILBERT H. EDWARDS, SR.

authorHOUSE·

AuthorHouse™
1663 Liberty Drive
Bloomington, IN 47403
www.authorhouse.com
Phone: 833-262-8899

Published by AuthorHouse 05/26/2021

ISBN: 978-1-6655-2760-6 (sc)
ISBN: 978-1-6655-2759-0 (e)

Print information available on the last page.

This book is printed on acid-free paper.

CONTENTS

PREFACE

This book has been prepared with common orders for the guidance of the family household. The author has focused on the idea of family in the household. There seems to be some confusion and uncertainty of how the family order works, such as the love of every member of the family and the role they play within the family.

The author feels that the man should know about the role, order, guidelines and relationships within the family household. Man has to know that God started the family, and He is concerned about the family. He created the ideal family household consisting of a husband, wife, son(s) and daughter(s). The author will try to point out and focus on the family and their household.

INTRODUCTION

Family living consists of a combination of roles played in various settings; in the Church, in the community, marriage in the family, etc. The author will attempt to point out subjects that will give a guideline for many who are concerned about the family.

The meaning of family; a group consisting of parents and children living together in a household. First, there must be a personhood: the image of God, which is the basis for defining human personhood. We are created with the capacity for relationships with God as the Creator, and with each other as fellow humans. This makes family life possible. The divine image makes family life possible. Divine image makes human beings different from all of God's other earthly creations.

Family Environment; the first chapters of Genesis introduce the theme of appreciation for the physical environment. (Genesis 2:4-17) Human life has been given an environment conducive to growth and entrusted with responsibility for using it well. Human marriages; God intended marriage to meet the basic need of love and companionship.

The first song in the Bible was sung by a man in joyous celebration of God's gift of a wife to him. The ideal marriage still produces this kind of rejoicing (Genesis 2:18; 20-25). From the very act of creation, unity within the marriage relationship is set forth in terms of oneness. The expression describing this companion literally means "a helper" alongside of him "a beautiful" description of the relationship, which God intended, between husband and wife (Genesis 2:18). One of God's purposes for marriage is companionship. Companionship; to help one another, are suitable or compatible for one another, and are able to stand alongside and share their personal lives. The unique quality of this companionship was demonstrated when Adam could not find a creature corresponding to himself among the animals that he was commissioned to name. The woman was built from a portion of the man's side, the suitable companion shares the same physical nature.

The basic implication of this text focuses on the similarity of man and woman, and on their mutual needs for each other. Because of their similarities, the man and woman can marry and establish one flesh union that takes priority over all other family relationships.

Chapter I

Family Personhood

Personhood means the quality or condition of being an individual person. It is the image of God that makes a person different. People are distinguished from the rest of God's animals that he created – in that they are His image. The Bible emphasizes that people are the creatures of God, the Creator. At the same time, life is passed on from parent to child in the normal life processes of conception and birth. Personhood comes before marriage. God brought every creature that He had made to Adam, but there was none suitable for him. Before marriage, the persons have to be of the same quality of being.

Human life is inherently social and needs human relationships for satisfactory development. Marriage is the fundamental response to this need, but more generally, human beings need interaction with other people in order to become whole persons. This speaks of Adam finding a suitable individual for him. Adam was looking for that personhood, which is the quality in that person. Adam did not take the first thing he saw, but he waited for the right mate.

In personhood, you look for that inward personality in that person. There is a need for good sense in a person. They must process a good character.

Love and faithfulness are two key biblical virtues. Love is a self-denying readiness to help other people. It represents a reciprocal relationship of service beyond social duties. Faithfulness indicates trustworthiness, reliability and loyalty. The work of love is to bring a smoothness in family relationships. Such love does not gloss over difficulty; rather, it provides the energy needed to bring the sometimes difficult results of forgiveness and reconciliation. Persons of integrity are marked by patience, slowness to anger and humility. Patience is the opposite of quick temper. A right understanding of love will usher in forgiveness and forgetfulness about an offensive act. Good character is shown by our ability to form friendships, or pattern of ethical living is to put off the negative and put on the positive. A positive person turns attention away from personal desires and achievements to relation with and needs of the family. Love is the center from which the family's attitude flows.

Self-control is a primary ingredient of family character. A person has the responsibility to choose the will to do the right and reject the wrong. The life of peace characterized by a spirit of forgiveness and reconciliation is to be a distinguishing facet of the person's life-style. This peace can be recognized by its application to prevent boiling over of quarrels into full scale breakdowns in relationships and by its continual presence in all day-to-day activities. Losing control affects our whole being. Gaining the control of your anger can provide a key to the maturing expression of a more positive virtue in your character. A person is obligated to learn God's moral expectations and obey them. Ethical behavior is rooted in strong personal devotion. Paul, in the book of Romans (12:12), is being transformed and making a thorough change in character.

Human beings are created to be like God. Some degree of physical likeness is implied by the use of identical terms to describe the likeness between Adam and the rest of creation. The divine image is of far more significance than this. However, it clearly includes authority and responsibility in so far as the natural world is concerned. The image of God may also be revealed in the male-female relationship of love and commitment. God is revealed through the loving commitment of one human being for another. God bestowed upon man the unique characteristics of Himself, by making them in His own likeness. Therefore, man and woman reflect and reveal the Creator's characteristics. God made man in His image to represent Him in the world. As human beings, we hold a special place of importance and service in God's perfect plan.

God wants man to be holy. Man is to strive for holiness and he shall be holy. God is demanding men to sanctify themselves. Israel is bidden to be holy (Leviticus 11:44). This demand has two aspects – one positive and the other negative. The positive aspect may be called the imitation of God, and the negative aspect means the withdrawal from things impure and abominable. It was the duty of the Israelites to strive, for as far as it was attainable by man, to avoid whatever would defile them, whether physically or spiritually. Whenever men and women honestly strive after holy living, such striving carries its own fulfillment with it. For I am holy; this constitutes the basis for your duty to sanctify yourselves, as well as the guarantee of your capacity to attain sanctification of life. Holiness is the very essence of the Divine being, and in breathing His spirit into you, He made you the partaker of His Divine and endowed you with the power to attain to holiness. "Because I am holy, you shall be holy, and you can be holy." God desires His people to become like Him in holiness. The path to holiness is in consecration, that is, cleansing from sin and dedication to God. By drawing near to God in this way, the holiness that characterizes God's nature will also characterize His people. Just as temple implement derived holiness from being dedicated to God's service, so people can have a holiness derived from God. God alone is Holy. Persons can be classed as holy only by participating in His holiness. When we are brought into a relationship with God, His holiness creates holiness in us in a purifying, sanctifying action. God's holiness makes stringent demands upon us. We must humble ourselves before Him and become marked with the qualities that mark His own life.

As God's creatures, we live under heavenly expectations of conduct. God places imperatives upon us which it is our duty to perform. As saints of God, we will walk through life with God. We also walk with other people, taking society's expectations into account. We must be righteous, living so, that the consequences of our actions bear just results for other people, both in the short term and over the long haul of life. Our ethical decisions include theological, social, relational and consequential aspects. Following God's moral expectations always carries the responsibilities of conveying these expectations to one's family. Our moral development begins through family habits and expectations through reading God's word.

Teaching and demonstration are part of God's mechanism to have character expectations placed before us. We are obligated to learn God's moral expectations and obey them. God set up moral demands on His people. His demands lead His people to be holy. God wants His people to learn at the outset of the vast qualitative difference between God and humans. God is holy, and we are not. People must humble themselves and purify themselves in the presence of a holy God. Human sin is the opposite of divine holiness. Sinfulness prevents us from looking upon the holiness of God. We must show respect for God and must come in the manner He prescribes. Those who appear in the presence of the Lord should show their respect in outward appearance, as well as, inward attitudes. The core attitude for stealing is coveting. The inner character damage done by coveting is severe. The society God intends for His people is based on love for neighbors (Exodus 20:17).

Lying, stealing, or any other dishonesty has no place among God's people. Each person is free to make moral choices. Those choices should be made within the responsible boundaries of what God has declared as moral or immoral. God's people must do what they know, and act on what they believe. Following God's guidelines for character includes acting with resolves and courage. Courage, as a biblical virtue, has parallels in perseverance, consistency and forthrightness. God's inspired word is the source for building godly character. We are called to follow biblical teachings. Obeying the word in total devotion to God is the essence of biblical ethics.

Personal character is not a secret. Those whom we associate with daily know our character. We need to hear their testimony and be ready to make necessary changes. We need teachers and role models to act as guides for our living tougher as God's people. We must wisely discern who the proper models are and follow them. Integrity of personal character finds its roots in a relationship with God (Job 31:1-40). Biblical ethics begin with two basic principles: (1) negative, evil life-styles should be rejected, and (2) peace or wholeness is the goal of life. We must proceed from rejecting evil to choosing and acting upon virtues, which are positive (Psalm 34:14). The promise of God's protection, blessing and joy reside with those who "love the Lord." To love Him is more than an emotion. It is a commitment to hate evil and avoid evil actions (Psalm 97:10-12). All of God's people should progress towards moral and spiritual perfection. God's company builds good character. Participation in evil practices with evil people destroys character (Psalm 141:4). We must exercise care in choosing the people with whom we identify. Friends help form our character. We do not choose friends to reform them. We want them to continue forming our character, leading us to righteous.

Love and faithfulness are two key biblical virtues. They are the focal point for the understanding and implementation of other virtues such as, peace, mercy, justice and righteousness (Proverbs 3:3,4). Character traits affect our physical health, as well as our relationship with God and man. Quick tempered, envy and oppression are foolish traits to cultivate. Patience is the opposite of quick tempered. Peaceful hearts do not envy others, and kindness leaves no room for envy.

Financial prosperity and social acceptance do not indicate that a person is successful in life or right with God. Commitment and strong personal relationships are more important. Building our lives around the moral expectations of God will produce a shield of encouragement against the insults of those alienated from God (Isaiah 51:7). We have a personal responsibility to refrain from the dangers of alcohol or any other addictive substance (Habakkuk 2:15).

The Sermon on the Mount summarizes Jesus' ethical teachings. It characterizes citizenship of His Kingdom. They meet expectations of behavior which go beyond a legalistic application of the moral law. The ethical standards that Jesus portrays are active in nature. God expects Christians to set these as standards for daily life (Matthew 5:1-7; 27). Anxiety over life is a perennial problem. Jesus' remedy for anxiety is to make the Kingdom of God and His righteousness the center of our proprieties (Matthew 6:25-34). In order to understand Jesus' instruction about humility, we must observe children. Their sense of innocence, directness and trust gives us keys to comprehending what is means to be humble in the Kingdom of God (Matthew 18:1-10). When a person is more concerned with what people think than what is right, preserving another's life is always more valuable than preserving your own reputation.

Evil character causes people to reject Jesus Christ. People are totally devoted in love to the darkness of the world's way, or they are ready to have their lives examined and changed by the Light of the world, Jesus. Persons devoted to evil fear what the light would reveal in their lives (John 3:19-21). Every person should be a person of prayer. Peter was a man of prayer. God uses praying persons to accomplish His will (Acts 10:9). Our model for living and source of will power for living is Jesus Christ. He was a perfect, sinless human being. He fulfilled the Law's requirement for atonement (Romans 10:4). Love people and be willing to do for them whatever you would do for yourself.

When a person's moral consciousness is weak or underdeveloped, innocent acts can appear wrong. If such a person commits that act, it has become a sin for that person and he or she is guilty (I Corinthians 8:7). Hold on, persevere, be faithful to the trust put in you, and have courage (I Corinthians 15:58). Christians should be strong, courageous and persistent. They are not abrasive and hardheaded (I Corinthians 16:13,14).

Enthusiasm adds spice to life. Enthusiasm must be a real, ongoing part of character; not a temporary act to impress other people. Love will act in discernment based on knowledge which broadens and deepens. Christian character shows itself in making the best decision for all concerned. Be full of thanksgiving towards God. Such attitude brings the sense of fulfillment and joy, in God that affects all of our relationships. This is God's peace, a peace so wonderful the human mind cannot fully understand it.

This peace can be a present reality for the person who gently and kindly lives life by letting God take care of anxieties (Philippians 4:4-7), to identify what is the will of God. Christians need consciously to think on the positive dimensions of life, being confident of his own standing with Jesus Christ.

The life of peace characterized by a spirit of forgiveness and reconciliation is to be a distinguishing facet of the Christian's life style. This peace can be recognized by its application to prevent boiling over of quarrels into full-scale breakdowns in relationships and by its continual presence in all day-to-day activities. Losing control affects our whole being. Gaining control of our anger can provide a key to the maturing expression of more positive virtues in our character.

CHAPTER II

FAMILY ENVIRONMENT

The first chapters of Genesis introduce the theme of appreciation for the physical environment. Bible positivity identifies God as the Creator of the earth and all that is within it. Human life has been given an environment conducive to growth and entrusted with responsibility for using it well.

God placed the newly created man in a garden especially created and designed as a comfortable home for him. God created the woman to be his companion, to share life with him in a complementary mutually fulfilling relationship. God desired for the man and woman a rich and full life. God expects them to live in the way of righteousness, which He set forth. The Tree of Life apparently represents the availability of eternal life for the couple in the garden. This relationship is forever. The first couple was made from and belonged to earth. They lost intimacy with God and cooperation with one another, and the environment.

God placed the man and woman in a good environment "The Garden of Eden", which became in the course of time, descriptive of any place possessing beauty and fertility. Later is was known as the "Heavenly Paradise", where the souls of the righteous repose in felicity. A Tree of Life was placed there; the fruit of which prolongs life, or renders immortality. The phrase also occurs in Proverbs 3:18, in a figurative sense; she is a tree of life to those who embrace her; those who lay hold of her will to be blessed.

After passing through the Garden, it divided into four separate streams. The Garden was in Eden, meaning according to the Hebrew word (delight), as I stated, the Tree of Life was in the middle of the Garden and also, the Tree of Knowledge of good and evil. A river flowed out of Eden to water the Garden, from there it divided and became four major rivers. The name of the first is Pishon. It surrounds the entire Land of Havilah where gold is found. The gold of that land is good. Also found there are pearls and precious stones. The name of the second river is Gibon. It surrounds the Land of Cush. The name of the third river is Tigris, which flows to the east of Assyria. The fourth river is the Euphrates.

After God created human beings (the man and the woman), He placed them in a very good environment for the first married couple. What could go wrong; only when bad, or evil comes in the midst. The family home should avoid all worldly actions. The family home should be a home that is dedicated to God. The children should be reared in a Christian home; not a home where sin dwells. The parents are to see that the home is free of sin, as much as possible. To fail to fulfill family responsibilities is sin; making one as untrue to the commitment of faith in Jesus Christ. The parents should provide necessities of life for their families. Biblical faith places a high priority on the family. Meeting the physical need of one's family is a part of Christian parenthood. Christians should manage personal resources in a responsible way to care for family needs.

Paul states that Christians are called to avoid all worldly actions (II Corinthians 6:16, 17). We cannot participate in worship and practices of other religious and/or philosophies because these would dishonor God. "Come out from among them, nor encourage or connive at any of their idolatrous or wicked practices." (Leviticus 11:44; I Peter 1:15, 16) Lot was told to leave Sodom and Gomorrah for they were wicked cities. Only Lot and his two daughters escaped the destruction of the two cities (Genesis 19:23-29). Lot's wife looked back (of the worldly things she left in Sodom and Gomorrah). She not only looked back, but lingered behind to be overtaken by the brimstone and fire from which the others escaped, and she became a pillar of salt.

God didn't want His people to stay in Egypt, in that environment. After the sojourn in Egypt, the contest with the Pharaoh and the Exodus, the Lord brought the people of Israel out of Egypt (Exodus 19:4-8). God desires His people to set themselves apart for His service. God told Moses to erect a sanctuary that shall be a visible emblem to the people that God dwelleth among them. The main purpose of the sanctuary was to wean the Israelites from idolatrous worship and turn them towards God. As God was holy, and as the sanctuary was holy, so must the Israelites make the sanctification of their lives the aim of all their endeavors. "I will meet with Thee;" The whole sanctuary is called "The Tent of Meeting." The place where God reveals His will, through Moses. God did not want the Israelites to stay in the environment Egypt. First John states, "Love not the world, neither the things in the world." This refers to all aspects of reality that are opposed to and separated from God; to get carried away by worldly lust is to move further from God and become a part of that which opposes Him. The environment in which we live leads us away from God to evil. God's Spirit leads us away from the world to Jesus Christ.

(I John 2:15-17)

Israel and Egypt; God and the world. Israel and Egypt represent two world-conceptions. Two ways of looking at God and man. For ages, Egypt was the land of wonder and men spoke in awe of the wisdom of the Egyptians. We know now that they were a wonderful people, but that is it only in the arts and crafts, and especially in their colossal and titanic architecture, that they attained truly astonishing results.

Israel, while in Egypt was yet but a child and was not strong enough to withstand Egypt in Egypt. Only out of Egypt could it grow uncontaminated by noxious influences of a decadent civilization. Only when liberated from the contagion of a nation of mere childish stammerers in the things of the spirit, could it flourish and fill the earth with the glad tidings of a God of holiness and pity, and the message of righteousness to men and nations.

Chapter III

Family Marriage

God intended marriage to meet the basic human need of love and companionship. The expression describing the companion literally means "a helper corresponding to him", or "a helper alongside of him"; a beautiful relationship which God intended between husband and wife. One of God's basic purposes for marriage is companionship.

The basic implication of the text focuses on the similarity of man and woman, and on their mutual need for each other. (Genesis 2:18-24) Because of their similarity, the man and woman can marry and establish a one-flesh union that takes priority over all other family relationships. In the early years of old, there was such a law as Covenant Marriage. Covenant; an agreement; Law; a contract drawn up by a deed. Theology; an agreement that brings about a relationship of commitment between God and His people.

The marriage of Isaac and Rebekah is a classic example of covenant marriage. Abraham, Isaac's father, wanted his son to marry a woman within the covenant community of

Israel and dispatched His trusted servant to go back to the town of Nabor to find such a wife. The covenant concept of marriage is not discussed at length in the Bible, but it is basic to an understanding of the meaning of marriage among the people of God. To covenant together as fellow believers in Jesus Christ is one of the grounds for stability in marriage (Genesis 24:1-67).

True human love involves and is based upon life commitment. It can also lead people to work long and hard to establish a lifelong relationship. True love leads to self-sacrifice. The relationship which should exist between husband and wife is one of complete giving of each other (Song of Solomon 2:16). When the husband and wife sins together, the marriage suffers (Jeremiah 44:19). When values are wrong and activities are sinful, the individual and the marriage suffers a long and close love for each other. When loss of a marriage partner, it may be the world's loneliest and saddest feeling, humans cannot provide sufficient comfort. I know that what I am about to say is not truly understandable; but infidelity does not always destroy the love of a faithful spouse. True love leads one to struggle to regain the love of the unfaithful one, paying whatever price that may be necessary (Hosea 3:1-3). Commitments in marriage can distract a person's commitment to Jesus Christ. For some it is better not to marry, than to get their lives so involved (I Corinthians 7:1-5). Also in critical times, marriage may become a distraction to service. Yet it must be clearly understood that neither celibacy nor marriage is necessarily better than the other, as a life style for serving God. A person's situation and need provides the criteria for determining whether to marry.

What is marriage? Marriage is that relationship between man and woman under whose shadow alone, there can be true reverence for the mystery, dignity and sacredness of life. Marriage is the conjunction of two loves in one mind. It shall first be explained what the nature of this conjunction is: the mind consists of two parts of which one is called "the understanding" and the other "the will." When these two parts act as one, they are called one mind. The husband acts the part which is called "the understanding", and the wife acts the part which is called "the will." When this conjunction, which is of the interiors, descends into the lower things that are of their body, it is perceived and felt as love. This love is conjunctive love. It is plain from this that conjugal love derives its origin from the conjunction of two in one mind. This is called cohabitation; however, it is said that they are not two, but one. For this reason, a marriage pair is not called two, but one.

There is such a conjunction of the husband and wife even in the inmost, who are of their minds, comes from creation itself. They who are in love, that is true conjugal, looks to what is eternal because there is eternity in that love. It being eternal is from the fact that love increases with the wife and wisdom with the husband to eternal. The husband must have wisdom and understanding of how to deal with his wife (I Peter 3:7). The prayer of the husband must not be hindered by misunderstanding in the relationship. The purpose of marriage is two-fold: posterity and companionship.

<u>Posterity</u>: the duty of building a home and rearing a family (Genesis 1:28) "Be fruitful and multiply." A childless

marriage was deemed to have failed of its main purpose and in ancient times, was admitted as grounds for divorce after ten years. In little children it was taught, God gives humanity a chance to make good of its mistakes.

Companionship: is the other primary end of the marriage institution. The woman is to be the helpmate of the man. A wife is a man's other self and all that man's nature demands for its completion physically, socially and spiritually. In marriage alone, can man's need for physical and social companionship be directed to holy ends? In marriage life, man finds his trust and most lasting happiness; and only through marriage life does the human personality reach its highest fulfillment. A man shall leave his mother and father, and cleave to his wife. A man who has no wife, abides without goodness, help, joy and blessings or atonement. Marriage is part of God's purpose in creation and should not be forbidden. Material things are not by nature evil. Neither are healthy sexual relationships of marriage, nor certain foods are sinful in themselves. God ordained marriage and procreation at creation. Everything He created was "very good." (Genesis 1:26)

Marriage and the family are ordered to the good of the spouses and to the procreation and education of children. The love of the spouses and the begetting of children create among members of the same family, personal relationships and primordial responsibilities. A man and a woman united in marriage, together with their children, form a family.

In creating man and woman, God instituted the human family and endowed it with its fundamental constitution.

Its members are persons equal in dignity. For the common good of its members and society, the family has manifold responsibilities, rights and duties. The relationships within the family bring an affinity of feelings, affections and interests, arising above all from the members' respect for one another. The family is a privileged community called to achieve a sharing of thought and common deliberation by the spouses, as well as their eager cooperation as parents in the children's upbringing, especially if you are Christians. Try to build up your marriage and home life in every possible way. Build each other up in personality and in happiness; and build up the personalities of your children by giving them a good example and an atmosphere of love and trust in your home. Deal with your children in an atmosphere of affection and unity.

Marriage calls for two kinds of love in order to bring fulfillment, rather than disappointment. It requires somewhat of the romantic love that drew you two together. Each must continue to feel that the other is special and precious. Each marriage is a personal relationship and it is what the two persons make it. Marriage is not merely feeling joy to each other. Tension in marriage is an outcome of being intense, and marriage is an intense affair. However, there is a way of living together which permits us to still remain tense and yet be relaxed towards each other. The purpose of two people in their marriage life is a joint purpose rather than a competition of independent purposes. In their major aims, they are one. Since their aims have the quality of mutuality, a part of the value of everything they do is that they do it happily together. When people are affectionately mature, the primary purpose of each is to being happiness to the other. Remember that as married, we are still lovers and should be resourceful in expressing our love.

Let's express our love, understanding and mutual respect in our tones, words and acts. Think of love as a gift from God, and at the same time, as an achievement in your lives together. Love is the true wealth of our home. Each person needs to come to a better understanding of who he or she is. Each person should find ways of how they should become more aware of his or her own thoughts, strengths, weaknesses, beliefs, values, feelings and fantasies. God has established and sanctified marriage. What God hath joined together, let no man put asunder.

Chapter IV

Family Sexual Nature

In God's creative purpose, human life is inherently sexual since maleness and femaleness define the physical nature of humans. Human sexuality describes all feelings about being a man or a woman that develops from infancy on through adult years. These feelings contribute to our understanding of masculine and feminine roles in marriage and family, as well as in all of society. Sexuality also refers to the various ways in which sexual desires are accepted and expressed in human relationships. Human sexual nature is God's idea and is to be used in accordance with His purposes for it. The woman was made from a portion of the man's side. Therefore, she is the feminine part that was taken out of man. She is being referred as physically weaker than man (I Peter 3:7). As it is known, in what the male and in what the female essentially consists of, this shall be briefly stated: The distinction consists essentially in the fact that in the make, the inmost is love and its vestment is wisdom. It is love over-veiled with wisdom; and that, in the female the inmost is that wisdom of the male, and its investment is the love there-from.

However, this love is feminine love and is given by God to the woman. Through the wisdom of the man, the former love that is masculine love, and is the love of being wise, given by the Lord to the man according to his reception of wisdom. There with it enables him to treat his wife according to knowledge. It is from this that the man is the wisdom of love, and that the woman is this love of that wisdom. It was from creation that in each, a love of conjunction into one was implanted and that the feminine is from the masculine, or that the woman was taken out of the man. The man is born into an affection for knowing, understanding, and being wise. The woman is born into the love of conjoining herself with that affection in the man.

Since the interiors form the exteriors to their likeness, the masculine form is a form of intellect and the feminine form is a form of the love of that intellect. So then, it is the man that has a different face, a different voice and a different body from the woman. That is to say, a harsher face, a harsher voice and a stronger body with a bearded chin. In general, a form less beautiful than the woman. They differ also in bearing and in manners. The man acts from reason and the woman acts from affection. The woman has a more, milder and beautiful face; a more tender voice and a more, softer body than man. There is a similar difference between the understanding and the will, or between thought and affection. The intelligence of woman, in itself, is modest, refined, pacific, yielding, gentle and tender; and the intelligence of man in itself is grave, harsh, unyielding, bold and fond of license. That such is the nature of woman and of man is very plain from the body. The countenance, the tone of voice, the speech, the bearing and manners of each. From the body in that men are hard and women are soft in skin and flesh. From the countenance in that the faces of men are harder, more resolute, rougher, tawnier and also bearded; therefore, less beautiful. The features of the woman are softer, more flexible, more delicate, lighter and therefore more beautiful. From the tone of voice, in that the tone of men is deep and the woman's tone soft. From the speech in that with men, it is fond of license and bold, and with women, modest and pacified. From the bearing, in that men are stronger and firmer, and with women, weaker and feebler. From the manners, in that with men they are more unrestrained, and with women more elegant.

Peter instructed Christian wives in voluntary submission to their husbands. For wives married to non-believers, devout behavior, may influence the husbands to become Christians. Christian husbands are to demonstrate their selfless giving love for their wives by honoring them, and showing them respect, since together, they are partners in the grace of life. (I Peter 3:1-7)

Man, (husband) and woman, (wife) should acknowledge and accept their sexual identity. Physical, moral and spiritual differences and complimentary are oriented toward the good of marriage and the flourishing of family life. The harmony of the couple and of society depends in part on the way in which the complementary needs and mutual support

22

between the sexes are lived out. In creating male and female, God gives man and woman an equal personal dignity.

Man is a person. Man and woman equally so, since both were created in the image and likeness of the personal God. Each of the two sexes is an image of the power and tenderness of God, with equal dignity though in a different way.

CHAPTER V

FAMILY COMPANIONSHIP

One of God's basic purposes for marriage is companionship. Companions help one another; are suitable or compatible to one another, and are able to stand alongside and share their personal lives with each other. Human life is inherently social and needs human relationships for satisfactory development. Marriage is the fundamental response to this need, but more generally, human beings need interaction with other people to become a whole person. Companionship cures loneliness. The whole created world was good. Creation of woman reinforced the overall goodness of creation. It was not good for man to be alone. Man was not evil, but he was incomplete and needed a helper for him. Companionship interacts, such as friendship does. Within the family of the Kingdom of God, Jesus' relationship with His disciples became one of friends loving each other. Friendship is a close, intimate relationship in which affection can be expressed freely. The heart of each friendship is the willingness even to give one's life for a friend. Families can develop friendships within the established role relationship of husband-wife, parent-child.

Just as Jesus and His disciples became friends, even though He never ceased being Lord.

Jesus exemplified just how friendship should be. Jesus called His disciples friends. Friends know the work of their master. He included them in His plans, and shared the responsibilities with them. Jesus makes His servants, His friends by trusting them, sharing His plans in love, and entrusting them with ministry (John 15:13-15).

Family ties should give family members freedom and encouragement to develop strong relationships outside the family, in spite of his father's anger. This fact illustrates the depth of commitment in true friendship and Saul's personal weakness in not freeing his son to enter the relationship openly. Family therapists indicate that families who have such friendships are generally happier in their own relationships (I Samuel 18:1-4).

Among the more precious human relationships are those where two people commit themselves one to another in the bonds and obligations of friendship. Jonathan became attached to David; Jonathan's soul was tied to David. Fellowship implies common likes, just as stated in I John 1:5-7. The darkness of sin has no part in God's existence. His own character sets the standard for what is right. He hates what is evil. His primary purpose, as He works in the world, is to overcome every sign of evil with His righteousness. We must realize that we cannot be in fellowship with God when we are doing or thinking those things that are evil. So, we should not do or think any evil of anyone that we have fellowship with. When the Church of Jesus Christ was born; Acts chapter 2; the believers devoted themselves to the Apostles' teaching and to fellowship with one another. The breaking of bread may refer to a regular fellowship meal, or refer to the Lord's supper.

Early Christian worship included teachings on the Old Testament and the experiences with Jesus, community fellowship and meals, prayer and praise. In the wilderness, God led Israel to construct a tabernacle as the central worship place (Exodus 25:8). God's purpose is to create a great family of free persons to be His own people. When people trust Jesus Christ as their savior, God pours His spirit into their hearts. The Spirit incorporates us into the common life of the Christian community. Jesus had prayed that His followers would be as united with each other as He was with the Father (John 17:20-23).

Baptism emphasizes the unity of Christian believers because they are baptized into one body, through one Spirit, by one faith in the one Lord Jesus Christ. That is why Paul exhorted the Ephesians to keep the unity of the Spirit through the bond of peace. If we do not keep the unity of the Spirit with our fellow believers in the body of Christ, we are contradicting what we confess in our baptism (Ephesians 4:5). I John states, "Have fellowship with us in our union and communion, through faith with the Father and the Son, that your joy may be full; by you being thus brought into full fellowship with God, and Jesus Christ. We must walk in the light to have fellowship (I John 1:6). Fellowship with one another; joyful communion with each other and with God (I Johnson 1:7). John put this in his writing to complete the fellowship of his audience with him and with the Father and Son. That complete fellowship, completed John's joy (I John 1:1-3).

Also, fellowship with God is exercised through prayer. Fellowship implies commonalities. We must realize that we cannot be in fellowship with God when we are doing or thinking those things that are evil. Salvation brings fellowship with other Christians and ethical living in the light of Jesus Christ's truth. The Spirit gives new life to those who put their faith in Jesus Christ. This new life is the life of God, and all Christians share it with one another. This is the fellowship of the Spirit. It is a single undivided fellowship. The Spirit gives gifts which help to strengthen the unity of God's family. People who work for the unity of the fellowship are guided by the Spirit. The Spirit leads the Christian fellowship in its great work of worship

(Jude 17-21).

Chapter VI

Family As One Flesh

Here, flesh refers to the whole human being rather than merely to the sensual or physical aspect of human nature. Becoming one flesh is established through sexual union, but the implications of the term are more than sexual. Sexual union creates a spiritual and psychological inter-relationship, in which the participants establish a bond that is more than physical. The one flesh union, therefore, establishes a bonding of personhood which is fundamental to marriage permanence. The one flesh union does not destroy the personhood of either partner, but celebrates the unity of their self-giving to each other in love. One flesh – dedicated love between marriage partners should bring fulfillment and contentment. The thought on sight of the beloved should flood the lover with happiness and joy. The result of shared love is contentment.

Sexual union is God's plan to create physical and emotional unity in the marriage relationship. Such unity is the foundation of the family. Participation in such union outside of the marriage commitment destroys family and betrays our commitment to Jesus Christ to whose body we belong and to whom we are united in spiritual union, as His bride. Sexual activity is not a right and/or need for every individual to be satisfied the easiest way possible. Sexual activity is a demonstration of commitment and unity within the family. (Genesis 15-17; I Corinthians 6:15-17)

Matthew 19:6 states, "…one flesh…"; they are so united as to be no longer two. But are each being a part of the other. The husband and wife are joined together in marriage to form a unique and single expression of life, as one flesh.

Paul teaches that the Church is the body of Christ. The saints are members of the one body. Each person was a member of Christ (I Corinthians 6:15-17). He has redeemed the bodies as well as the bodies, as well as the souls of believers. As such, they are spiritually united to him now, and shall be throughout eternity, he that is joined unto the Lord is one spirit; one spirit with Christ. Christ dwells in Him and he in Christ. This mutual union makes him spiritual, as Christ is spiritual. Paul states in Ephesians 2:11-22, that all race, culture, tradition and geography come together as one. In Jesus Christ, God broke down all human barriers and created the Church as one body of sinners in relationship to one another and to Him.

The Church unites all believers from all races and locations in a common ministry in Jesus Christ and a common hope for Jesus Christ's return (Ephesians 3:6). Paul speaks of the mystery of redemption. The mystery is that God is calling out the Gentiles and making them heirs with Israel; making them into one body in Jesus Christ. As God is one, so is the

Church. To serve Jesus Christ, the Church must maintain its unity. Each member must serve in gentle, humble love, seeking peace and unity with every other member. The one spirit in our lives lead us to be one Church, not a Church with divisions and splits. (Ephesians 4:1-6)

Baptism emphasizes the unity of Christian believers because they are baptized into one body through one spirit, by one faith, in the one Lord Jesus Christ. The unity of the spirit in the bond of peace; be united in affection and live in peace, according to the leading of the Holy Spirit. One body; the Church, the body of Jesus Christ, of which all true believers are members. One Spirit, one Holy Spirit dwelling in the hearts of all, and animating all. One hope, hope of heaven, through faith in the divine redeemer; one Lord; Jesus Christ. One faith; in respect to both its object, its origin, and its inward character. It is faith in the one gospel of Jesus Christ; it is wrought in our souls by the one Spirit of God; and it is one in its nature and effects, being a faith which works by love, purifies the heart and overcomes the world. One baptism; for all are baptized into one Savior. The Church responds to Jesus Christ as a loving wife responds to a loving and kind husband. Jesus Christ gave Himself on the cross for His Church to set the Church apart, as His unique people living in service to Him. He is now cleaning the Church that is might be presented to Him as a purified body; because we are members of His body. (Ephesians 5:25-32)

Chapter VII

Family Childbearing

Bearing and nurturing children is one of the biblical purposes for marriage and sexuality. Sexual intercourse makes conception possible, but ultimately conception and birth depend on "the help of the Lord." (Proverbs 5:15-19) Both men and women valued children as God's blessing to their marriage (I Corinthians 7:3-5). Childbearing is still a fundamental purpose for marriage, but planning the time and number of children is consistent with responsible Christian parenthood (Psalm 127:3-5; 128:3-6; I Samuel 1:18-20). Controlling conception is not discussed in the Bible. Being fruitful (Genesis 1:28), does not demand unlimited reproduction. Children add riches and joy to life. They do not represent human achievements for the parents, but blessings from God. Grandchildren bring joy and hope to aging adults (Psalm 128:3-6). Loyal children are parents' greatest blessing. Families should be characterized by a feeling of gratitude and blessings for each family member. Upright children are the reward of parents own righteous behavior. One who raises children while he still has the strength to guide them is then credited for their accomplishments; and when the children are raised in his youth, they are his help as time goes by. Happy are the parents who raise such children. "Your wife will be like a fruitful vine in the inner recesses of your house." The wife will behave with modesty within her house. When the wife is like a fruitful vine, so then your children will be life olive saplings. (Psalm 128:3)

The make-up of a birth; both male and female have 23 pairs of chromosomes. In the male, one of the pairs is of unequal length. The larger chromosome of this pair is called the "X" and the smaller is called the "Y". Females have 2 "X" chromosomes in their karyotype. The "X" and "Y" chromosomes are called the sex chromosomes, because they carry genes that determine the sex in humans. A human processes 46 chromosomes or 23 pairs of chromosomes. These pairs are called homologous chromosomes. During meiosis, the homologous chromosomes separate. In this way, each daughter cell will receive half the total number of chromosomes, but one of each kind. Half of the chromosomes' total number is necessary to keep the chromosomes' number constant from generation to generation.

Each sperm and egg has only 23 chromosomes, so that after the fertilization, the new individual has 46 chromosomes. By way of the gametes, each parent contributes one chromosome of each homologous pair of chromosomes in the new individual. Therefore, when the woman was formed from the man, God created another new being in total, modifying some of the chromosomes. God made male and female one in marriage, since it takes both of them to bring one new life into the world. God said unto them, "be fruitful and multiply and replenish the earth." (Genesis 1:28)

The birth of children is the natural and expected outcome of human marriage. Each person born develops individual characteristics and personalities, not being merely a copy of either parent or of other family members.

The story of Jesus' birth emphasizes His unique nature as a human child and son of God. The genealogy or list of human ancestors show the human side of Jesus and corrects Him through Joseph to David and Abraham, with whom God had special covenants to achieve His redemptive purpose (Matthew 1:18). The virgin birth emphases Jesus' divine nature since Mary was with child "through the Holy Spirit." Mary is described as having had no "union" with Joseph. She was with child through the "Holy Spirit."

The virgin birth was God's chosen way to become incarnate: the invisible, spiritual God became human. In this miraculous birth, God is the Father, who is directly responsible for the creation of Jesus' body (Hebrews 10:5).

Chapter VIII

Family Childhood and Youth

Youthful dreams are a normal part of the process of growing up. Some dreams (like those of Joseph) may be revelatory. Unfortunately, in Joseph's case, the recounting of his dreams flamed the resentment already present due to parental partiality. Only the passage of time can determine the true nature of adolescent dreams (Genesis 37:2-11).

Dealing with the profound thoughts in terms of everyday life, a child can grasp the outline of the story of Joseph. Yet, the greatest thinkers are continually finding in it fresh depths of unexpected meaning. Like Summer and the starry skies, like joy and childhood, these stories touch and enthrall the human soul with their sublime simplicity, high seriousness and marvelous beauty. And, they are absolutely irreplaceable in the moral and religious training of children. After having repented for three thousand years and longer, these stories still possess an eternal freshness to children of all races and colors.

Joseph, being seventeen years old, used to supervise-although only a lad-his brethren, the sons of Bilhab and the sons of Zilpath, when they were with the sheep. Benjamin was but an infant, and the father's affections were centered on Joseph. When Joseph was sold, Jacob's whole life was bound up with Benjamin. To his father, Joseph is at first the clever child of a large family, too untutored in life to veil his superiority. I will end this story in Genesis 45:15, after that, the brethren did not talk to him until he had shown the same fraternal love to them as he had done to Benjamin. Then they knew that his heart was with them.

Parents are responsible for dedicating their children to the Lord. Children should grow up with the awareness of devotions by parents to the purposes of God (I Samuel 1:21-28). Youth is the time of great expectations. To have to face death at such a time is an exceptional tragedy. Psalm 88:16 – no trouble or tragedy is horrible enough to separate us from God. Youth is a time of development and experimentation. The young should find satisfaction in their youth, but must recognize they are still responsible to God for all their youthful acts. While not to be belittled, undue value should not be placed upon youth as such. A generation which strives for youthfulness has missed the point of life itself, for youth is only an introductory stage of life (Ecclesiastes 11:9-10).

Here in Jeremiah 1:6,7, indicates immaturity mere likely referring to a young person, than a child. Immaturity makes people feel inadequate to the tasks of adulthood. Immaturity must never be misconstrued as inability. God enables people of every age to do what He calls them to do (Jeremiah

1:6,7). Parents and teachers should study the children. The needs of the children require it. The word "education" comes from a world meaning "to lead out." To lead the child out to meet the experiences of life in a way that will bear him. God's word is to lead the child to feel, to think, and to do right, to himself, to his fellow-men and his God – this is the privilege of every parent and teacher. Teaching then, is causing another to feel and to know the right in order to do it. The parent and teacher should know about the child. Through the study of the child, the parent and teacher will learn the general characteristics of the child in the various stages of development, that he may realize that children of various ages require different treatment. The infant cries to get the attention he needs or the thing he craves. The child's demand for toys and the truants running away are but the same kind of warning that either the intellect or heart is being starved. If the parent or the teacher understands this and the demands of nature are supplied, the work of the parent or teacher will be preventive, rather than, corrective. The child's wriggling, the boy's boisterous laugh and the giggling of the girls have their causes in natural places of development. These should be properly interpreted, instead of being crushed.

Many children have been ruined because parents and teachers have misunderstood their actions. There are two types of children: <u>the motor child</u> – like the motor of the car, is easy to start, but makes considerable noise in starting; then he is swift to travel and quite attractive, but may also stop just as suddenly as he started. Impulsive and enthusiastic, he is quick to comprehend and to decide, but is as quick to change his mind. Action precedes deliberation. He acquires knowledge readily and forgets even more easily. The <u>sensory child</u>; is quiet and thoughtful, slower to respond, but steady when turned. He is possibly less attractive at first, but he wears well. It is more difficult for him to acquire knowledge, but he retains for a longer time what he has learned. The parent or teacher can study the child by watching him; how he is rewarded and punished; how he is taught; the motives that appear to him; whether he obeys from fear or love. How is the atmosphere of the home? The parent or teacher should love the things the child loves, if you can do so with propriety and make him love you. Therefore, establishing sympathy. Study the things about which he knows, and connect your lesson with those things. See him play his games and have him explain his toy. Judge him fairly and gain his confidence. When the child plays, he uses up surplus energy. The child who has been compelled to remain quiet and attentive has stored up energy, which unless he has an outlet, will force out the cork and damage something. If the child leaves the room where he was compelled noisily and yells in the corridors and in the neighborhood, it is because his play energy must have an outlet. Play trains the body for the future. Swimming, ball games, skating and other games develop the muscles, and the fresh air and sunshine build for the child a reliable constitution for his adult life mentally; that is developed through the use of the senses in play. The child becomes alert and his judgment is trained. Moral, justice, unselfishness and loyalty are virtues that may be attained through play.

The infant is an investigator. He hunger senses are being fed by new sights, sounds and tastes, which furnish him with the basis for future knowledge. He pulls, twists and tares everything he can lay his hands on. This is not because he is mischievous, but because he is obeying that spirit of investigation. The child; he longs for playmates with whom he can match his skill. His games require more skill and knowledge than the plays of infants. He is an imitator; the girl plays house; the boy pretends to be a policeman or a fireman. The youth; he has the gang instinct. He joins the club and wears the club uniform and badges. He likes games that call for teamwork; such as football, basketball and baseball.

Chapter IX

Family Female Subordination

Female subordination is introduced into the one flesh relationship that previously (Genesis 1 and 2), had been one of shared authority over the physical world. The judgement on Eve included increased pain in child-bearing and subordination to the husband, for whom she had desires that leads to child-bearing. Since Eve had not yet given birth, this judgement explains the pain associated with joy of becoming a mother. The condition that her sexual desire be for her husband alone, influenced some interpreters to propose that sexuality was in some way involved in the fall. It is probable that this condition is related to the previous one on child-bearing. Even though child-bearing is associated with pain and pregnancy as a result of sexual union, the wife is to continue to desire sexual relations with her husband. Since Eve had refused to obey God's instructions given through Adam, he was to rule over her. Such subordination was not in the original purpose of God for marriage, but it is a consequence of Eve's failure to obey God.

The relationship of the Gospel to the "Fall", to submission, and to marriage is basic to an understanding of the husband-wife relationship, as taught in the New Testament (Ephesians 5:2), the fear of the woman gaining the upper hand over man, if not forced into submission. It's apparent that the King was drunk, and wanted to put Queen Vashti on display, when he sent servants to bring her into the banquet hall. Her refusal was not based upon stubbornness, but propriety. She did not want to be a spectacle. The fact of her refusal aroused the King's anger, and created tension from his advisors. Fearful that other wives would follow her example, they decreed that every man should be the ruler in his household. The text states two principles: (1) a wife is not wrong to refuse her husband's will, when it would make her do that which she believes is wrong for herself, and (2) fear of women becoming dominant may lead men to take actions that are ill-advised and inappropriate to the circumstances involved (Esther 1:10-22).

Paul states in I Corinthians 11:3; "The head of the woman is the man." Head – rightful governor or ruler. So the woman shall be subject to the man. It is the will of God that there should be a difference of condition, and this requires a difference in their appearance. In the old biblical times, the custom or tradition was that the woman should have her head covered. Verse 5; Dishonoreth her head; her husband's, by appearing as if she were not in subjection to the man. Verse 6; "Let her be covered" veiled as a token of subjection to man. Verse 7; the glory of man; her excellence is an expression of his dignity and worth, since she was formed of him and for him. Verse 10; Power, that is a veil, as the token of her husband's rightful authority over her, and of her subjection to him.

Adam was first formed; an indication that he is the head of the woman (I Timothy 2:13), and the office of teaching and governing belongs to the man. (I Corinthian 11:8,9)

Chapter X

Family Education

The household in Biblical times included the primary family, servants, other family members and persons entrusted with various responsibilities for maintaining the household. In the household of Abram, children of servants were educated as soldiers from their youth (Genesis 14:14; Proverbs 4:1-7).

Education is a basic task of the household. Parents are responsible for providing religious and moral instructions to their children. This is God's given responsibility and is to be taken as seriously as the obligation to provide food, clothing and shelter. When parents neglect this teaching task, God is forgotten, values become corrupt and society as a whole suffers decline (Deuteronomy 6:1-10; Genesis 18:19). Nurturing the faith of children through God-centered teaching is one of the greatest privileges of parenthood. It is also a sacred obligation. The task cannot be done on an occasional basis. It must be a continuous process – morning, noon and night (Deuteronomy 6:1-10). The Word of God is to be quoted, explained, discussed, symbolized and written down. Most importantly, it is to be "written upon the heart" and incorporated into the parents' way of life, so the children may have a daily example of godly living (Proverbs 1:8-9)

All Christian parents need God's guidance in the nurturing and education of their children. Though scattered and persecuted, the Jews have managed to maintain their ethnic and religious identify from ancient times until the present day. One of the important reasons for this perseverance lies in their continued teaching of the faith from one generation to another (Psalm 78:1-6). The first and most important classroom in the school of life is the home. Both the father and mother are to assume the responsibility for training and nurturing the minds of their children. Though school and church might contribute significantly to the process of education, no outside agency can equal the influence of parents, as an educative force.

Parents must discipline their children in order for the children to have a chance in life. Without discipline and correction, we never learn, (Proverbs 13:1,24; 19:18; 22:15; 23:13-14; 29:15-17). Being in infancy, human beings learn by imitating the behavior of others. The examples that others set are not always positive. The biblical writer had this in mind, when he warned against association with persons who are habitually angry. Negative emotions are contagious. Children whose parents are temperamental have no choice in the matter. Brought up under the daily influence of angry parents, they learn to be hot-tempered persons themselves. By self-discipline, and associating with the right people, we can unlearn bad habits acquired as children. We cannot blame our problems on our parents. We must take responsibility for ourselves and set good examples for our families, friends and associates (Proverbs 22:24-25).

Responsibility for nurturing children in the faith is fixed on the shoulders of the fathers, (Ephesians 6:4). Mothers will have much to do with the nurturing and training of children, but the fathers who relinquish this duty entirely to their wives do so in clear violation of the New Testament teaching. "Training" in the Greek language means a combination of instruction, discipline and personal guidance. Fathers are also warned against engendering anger and frustration in their children. Ephesians 6:4 – "Provoke not your children", give them no just occasion to be angry, or to feel as they were injured, as the highest good of children in this life requires them in all things right to obey their parents. It is the duty of the parents to take the course which is best suited to secure this, and lead their children also to obey their Father in Heaven. In order to do this, they obey Him themselves, daily seek His guidance and blessing, instruct their children to do His will, and present to them the motives which He has revealed. They must also accustom their children, from their earliest years, to promptly submit their will to the will of their parents, so that it shall by habit become easy and pleasant. Timothy's early training under the guidance of a godly mother and grandmother was a precious heritage (I Timothy 4:6). This training made him a good minister or servant of Jesus Christ and His church. It has molded not only Timothy's thinking, but his life (II Timothy 1:5).

The Sunday School is not a substitute for the home. The Sunday School teacher cannot take the place of the parent, and assume the responsibility of father or mother. The effort of good Sunday-school teaching should be to encourage the parents to facilitate in home training. Sunday-school teaching should add to the effectiveness of home teaching. When home teaching is lacking, the school should make up for the lack. The home has a right to insist that the instructions of the children shall themselves be sincere Christians. When teaching a child, love the things he loves, if you can do so with propriety, and make him love you. Study the things about which he knows, and connect your lesson with those things. See him play his games; have him explain his toy. Judge him fairly and gain his confidence. God wants the parents to teach the children.

Teaching is imperative, not optional. Where teaching is rejected, spiritual amnesia sets in. Parents (Deuteronomy 6:1-10), and spiritual leaders play essential roles in this education process. God dealt with Israel in the Book of Deuteronomy 4:9,10,14. The survival of the nation depended on Israel's memory of and loyalty to the Law of Sinai from thy memory; the "heart" being conceived as the seat of memory. Make them known unto thy children. These things must also be kept alive in the memory of posterity, so that future generations do not lose their spiritual identity and sink back into heathenism.

This transcendent duty towards children and children's children is repeated with the utmost emphasis throughout Deuteronomy. Such insistence on the sacred obligation of religious education led to the first effort in the world's history to provide elementary instructions to all the children of the community.

Deuteronomy 6:7, teaches them diligently; prick them in; so that the words remain indefinitely upon their hearts. Let them have a clear, and not confused or stammering knowledge of the duties and teachings of their faith. They are to be a theme of living interest, early and late, at home and abroad. A man should conduct himself with due propriety in his house, so as to set an example to his household, and he should also be gentle with them and not overwhelm them.

All children need guidance to stay on the right path. So long as the Priest Jehoiada instructed Joash in the way of the Lord, King Joash remained in God's will. After the death of his teacher, Joash became very wicked (II Kings 12:2).

Genuine education goes back to the basic sources of knowledge, and the Lord is the fundamental source of all knowledge and wisdom (Job 28:28). True wisdom produces a moral life, not just an admired mind (Psalm 14:1). The Psalmist states the long range perspective of his people when he stressed the importance of teaching not only the next generation, but even the children of those who are not yet born (Psalm 78:1-6). The godly person does not depend upon previous learning to keep walking in the way of truth, but upon God's continued guidance. The child of God never graduates from the school of divine instructions. The happy, secured individual learns from life's difficult experiences and acknowledges that God's law points to discipline for the disobedient. Parents, don't spare the rod (Proverbs 23:13,14). Parents can spare their children from grief later in life, if they will correct and guide them in their younger years (Proverbs 19:18). Parental discipline should always be corrective in nature, never vindictive. Parenthood can contribute to trouble and unhappiness in the lives of children, and sometimes even to their untimely death. Even if your efforts to discipline your child do not seem to be bearing fruit, do not be dissuaded. There is still hope that, if you persist, your message will eventually seep in. However, under no circumstance may you even consider putting an end to him because of his weaknesses, or while spanking may be a valuable educational tool, it must be used sparingly.

A necessary responsibility of parents is disciplining children (Proverbs 23:13-16). The training prepares them for life and brings satisfaction to the parents. Proverbs stresses the importance of mothers as teachers in the home, with all her other laudable traits. The ideal woman pictured in this passage is also an excellent teacher (Proverbs 31:26). Parents as teachers, and all other teachers should be as God; as the teacher of His people. God is gentle and loving, like a father helping a toddler take his first steps (Hosea 11:3). Be yourself when you teach. Hypocritical teaching is worse than no teaching at all. Teachers who are pious on the outside, but corrupt on the inside, can delude those who follow them, leaving them worse off spiritually than they were before.

Parables were powerful teaching tools in the hands of the master teacher, Jesus Christ. The parables of Jesus are among the best known stories in the world. Though they are stories about everyday things, they pierce to the very heart of spiritual truths. As teachers, we need to use stories from everyday life to help students, (also children in the home), see the radical effects that Christian faith should have in our lives (Mark 4:2). Parents should follow the example of the bible on how to educate their children; asking and answering questions are one of the most ancient educational methods in the world, played an important role in the religious instructions of First Century Jewish boys. In the temple scene, Jesus was not "grilling" His teachers, but was asking for information. Question asking should not be the exclusive prerogative of teachers; it is important for learners to raise questions too, (Luke 2:46). The key to living a transformed life is cultivating a renewed mind. The Christian, who is too lazy mentally to drink deeply from God's revealed word or to think courageously about the meaning of personal faith will tend to be shaped by institutionalized values and socially acceptable modes of thought. The study desk and the prayer closet are both essential to Christian teaching and learning. Teachers serve learners' needs rather than satisfy personal ego problems.

Chapter XI

Family Multiple Wives

Abram's taking of Hagar as a concubine upon Sarai's instructions result in hostility between Sarai and Hagar. Sarai acted upon her disbelief in God's promise of a son and gave her handmaiden to Abram, so that she might bear a child in Sarai's stead. Using a servant girl as a concubine was common among the patriarchs of Israel, (Genesis 16:1-16). She remained a slave, but any children born from her union with her master had the same status as a child born to the legitimate wife. It was not uncommon for a man who had no heirs to have children by a concubine in order to keep his family name alive. Having multiple wives was not based upon any specific word of God. Such polygamy was practiced by the leaders and Kings of Israel and Judah with Solomon having the largest number of wives and concubines. The historical examples are never set up as authoritative instructions from God's people in all generations to follow. One spouse for a lifetime is the biblical teaching (Genesis 16:1-16).

Neither political strategy nor community acceptance justifies sinful behavior. Marriages cemented political alliances for Solomon. The community saw his actions as good politics. The marriages introduced false religions to Israel. God saw them as sin (I Kings 11:1-9). It is written biblically that "He must not take many wives, or his heart will be led astray", (Deuteronomy 17:17). Rehoboam's imitation of his father's sin does not excuse him from guilt (II Chronicles 11:18-21). One of the reasons for having multiple wives was in the Ancient Orient, childlessness was a calamity and disgrace to a woman. That is why Sarai gave her handmaid to Abram, her husband. It was the legalized custom in Babylon, the homeland of Abram and Sarai, that if a man's wife was childless, he was allowed to take a concubine, but he was not to place her upon an equal footing with his first wife. The same, also, happened to Jacob with Rachel, when Rachel could not give Jacob children (Genesis 29:31-30:24). In the New Testament, (I Timothy 3:2) a Bishop must be the husband of one wife.

King Solomon loved foreign women. I Kings 11:2; God had told the Israelites, "Do not intermarry with them, and do not let them intermarry with you; lest they turn your heart away to follow their gods." They must not come among you. Do not let them participate in public affairs, even after converting. This was Solomon's transgression, for the marriages themselves could be justified on political grounds. During the time of Paul, Christians were very few. The number of converts increased daily, but many of the new comers into the Church of Christ were polygamists. When they embraced Christianity, they could not easily put their wives away.

(I Timothy 3:2) The husband of one wife, refers to an elder who has only one wife. The Church would not have selected a Christian elder with three or four wives. Family quarrels and troubles would have weakened his reputation.

Jesus made no attack on polygamy, but told His disciples that from the very beginning, God had created man, male and female. He seemed to take it for granted that a man should have only one wife. He once said, "For this cause shall a man leave Father and Mother, and shall cleave to his wife; and they twain shall be one flesh." (Matthew 19:5)

Chapter XII

Family Conflicts

There shouldn't be conflict in the family home. Conflict; a se

rious disagreement or argument. The family of Isaac and Rebekah demonstrates sibling rivalry and parental favoritism as illustrations of family conflict (Genesis 25:19-34). Jacob shrewdly conned his twin brother Esau into selling the birthright which was legitimately Esau's, because he was the first born. Later, Rebekah contrived with Jacob to deceive Isaac, who favored Esau. Isaac loved Esau and Rebekah loved Jacob. Each parent had a favorite child which led to the breakup of the household. "Love thy children with an impartial love."; is the wise admonition of a medieval Jewish teacher. Even among Christians, conflict can develop in family relationships. Christian families should go to God for His grace of forgiveness and strength in seeking to bring harmony and reconciliation to family life.

God's elective plan (Genesis 25:3) – custom places the older son in family leadership, even when the brothers are twins. God's election chose the younger son to carry out

His covenant purpose. The election conflict with customs introduced a life of conflict for Jacob. But still, everyone has life's problems.

In the book of Judges 16:4-22, is the story of Sampson and Delilah. The destructive effects of deceit and quarreling on personal relationships is exemplified in the tragic experience with Sampson and Delilah's life. Sampson was apparently drawn primarily by sexual attraction. Delilah showed no concern for his welfare when offered money to betray him. Relationships based on feelings such as this has little chance for survival. Only faithful commitments can overcome conflicts and competing loyalties.

Too often, religion becomes a source of marital conflict, such as in David and Michal's marriage (II Samuel 6:16; 20-23). Michal was disgusted with David's behavior while he was accompanying the Ark of the Lord on its return to Jerusalem. She felt that it was inappropriate for the King to be dancing and singing in the street. David justified his behavior on the basis of his devotion to the Lord. Marriage partners in a conflict situation often use religion to justify actions the mate dislikes. Unequal religious devotion can also cause marital conflict. Micah 7:5-6, describes a family conflict during the troubled times of God's judgment on Israel's sinfulness. Family members could not trust each other. Self-preservation became more important than family commitment. Sin, distrust and self-centeredness lie at the center of family conflicts. Families cannot function without deep communication and trust. Anger is a response to disappointment, frustration, blocked plans, or personal putdowns that happen from time to time in family homes. Anger can be buried inside a person or expressed in attacking the one toward whom anger is directed.

Conflict Resolution

The positive approach is to resolve anger, so that it will not build up to an explosion or poison the inner being by becoming resentful. Paul (Ephesians 4:26-27), advised Christians to recognize their anger, deal with the issues that cause it and resolve it before going ot bed. When anger is internalized and stored up, it becomes resentment, which gives an opportunity for the devil to work in your heart. Sometimes, family members be in anger without or beyond just cause; or by indulging it too long, with a wrong spirit, or for a wrong end. Don't listen to the wrong spirit within you, who will tempt you to hate such as to injure you, and to seek revenge. Christian families also have problems; it is wrong to allow them to go on with letting the teaching of God's word help bring about resolution of conflict.

Chapter XIII

Family Relationships

Jealousy between children, plus parental partiality, breeds dishonesty and deception. The consequences are a divided family, frequently produce hatred, lack of trust, and dissolution of the family (Genesis 27:1-40). Deep and divisive problems, within a family, leads members to substitute rejection for acceptance. Acceptance is the only basis for family life. Rejection frequently simmers below the surface until grief or loss brings it to the light. Respect and love for parents often keeps the lid on such rejection until the parent's death. Rejection and hatred of others establishes the foundation for the possibility of more violent acts. The ultimate in loving commitment is realized when one person offers to bear the punishment of another.

The normal loving relationships within a family can be used by God even when the people involved are unaware of it (Exodus 2:1-10). Family relationships can be used to aid family member in serving God. Moses received his inspiration direct from God; and becomes the inspirer of his brother, who acts as his interpreter to Pharaoh and Israel. The basis for a stable society is a stable family. A stable family must be built upon respect for life, property, sexual commitments and trustworthiness. Personal contentment furnishes the basis for this kind of stability. In the Old Testament times, the family line was thought to be transmitted only through sons. But now, neither sons or daughters should not be penalized for their parents' sin (Numbers 27:3-4).

God's love is not like the love of a mortal father. He that created the world extends His love to all His children; not like that of the Old Testament, that the father's love is only for his sons. The sins of any one person seriously affects and can have serious consequences for each member of a person's family. Everyone should suffer for their own sins. Also, it will seriously affect those closet to them (Joshua 7:20-25).

One of the more difficult family situations is that of being torn because two people closely related to us has made opposing demands. When obedience to parents becomes opposed to the bonds of love and friendship with others, one relationship must be sacrificed for the other. Fear destroys many family relationships. Fear makes enemies of people who should love and help one another. Don't let fear come between your relationships. God intends people to live in families. Human nature has a deep need to be related to other people in a loving and secure relationship. Destroyed relationships create barriers between family members. God's word calls us to maintain good relationships with others. Members of the family need the strength of a few solid relationships rather than a large number of superficial ones which offer no support (Proverbs 18:20-24).

The maintenance of family relationships is the responsibility of each member of the family. Bad family relationships destroy its members. The family should teach us cooperation through shared responsibilities and joint projects. Family ties are supposed to bind people together. When hatred breaks such ties, the tragedy is extreme. People expect to be able to trust family members. When that trust is betrayed, we are overwhelmed. Family relationships are important. But there are times when we must choose between family relationship and a relationship with God. Too often we trust human solutions to our crisis rather than trusting God. Edom and Israel were descended from the two brothers, Esau and Jacob. To deny or betray such a relationship was a violation of family commitment and a denial of family responsibilities (Obadiah 10:12). Families ought to be able to trust one another. The closer the relationship between family members, the greater should be the degree of trust. Refuges afraid to return home represent one of our world's greatest tragedies. Broken human relationships and oppression forces the families to become refuges (Matthew 2:13). Anger destroys family relationships. At the very least, it destroys compassion; at the worst, is can threaten life itself (Matthew 5:21-22).

There should not be pride in the family. Pride destroys relationships between families. It also hinders the relationship between people and God. When pride is cast aside for an attitude of childlike humility, these relationships can stand. Family expects one another to help them in an emergency. Failure to do so may destroy or deny friendship. Families should be fundamentally concerned. They should live in the sensitive awareness of the weaknesses of others so they do not lead another into sin. Family members need to know that family members can have destructive consequences in family members. Family members should accept one another without passing judgment on them. They can still love one another even while disagreeing, so not to give satan a foothold through division. If families act in a way they know will offend a family member, they have done wrong. Families must live so as to encourage family members rather than offend them. The ideal relationship between family is that of self-giving love. This love is founded upon a proper relationship with God and with oneself.

CHAPTER XIV

FAMILY DISOBEDENENCE

Disobedience; failure or refusal to obey rules or someone in authority. By Hebrew Law, if a man dies and leaves no children, his brother was required to marry the widow and father children who would bear the name of the deceased brother. Under the patriarchal family structure of that time, neither the widow nor the brother could refuse the demand of the head of the family to fulfill this obligation. So Onan took Tamar as a second wife and had intercourse with her, but withdrew before ejaculation in order that she not become pregnant. He did not want to father a child that would not bear his own name. This disobedience resulted in his death (Genesis 38:1-10). Onan sinned by refusing to fulfill his duties to his brother's wife according to the tradition of his people and later biblical law. People rebel against moral limits. God responds to continual rebellion by letting people carry their moral freedom of choice to absurd limits. Evil becomes the standard operating procedure for such people. Even in the face of death resulting from their rebellion, they continue devoting themselves to immorality.

The lose the ability to distinguish between right and wrong; being death to God's voice. The human mind makes the free choice to ignore God and follow its own wisdom. In doing so, it lets fleshly lust dominate, rather than let the spiritual strive to know God. Such an intellect leads people astray, causing the rejection of God Himself and leading to wholly irresponsible behavior (Romans 1:28-32).

In Deuteronomy 25:5; Levirate marriage is the technical name for the marriage with the widow of a childless brother. To avert the calamity of the family line becoming extinct, of a man's name perishing and his property going to others, the surviving brother of such a childless man required to marry the widow; so as to raise up an heir to that man's name. This custom existed in Israel in patriarchic times; in Genesis 38, where it states: perform the duty of a husband's brother. This refers to the custom of the Levirate marriage by which a surviving brother-in-law marries the childless widow (Deuteronomy 25:5 and Ruth 4:5). The eldest son of such marriage inherits the name and property of the deceased.

Ruth 3:1-4 and 12 states; marriage to a widow of an Israelite involved intricate covenant regulations, and it must be obeyed. Boaz showed loyalty to God's covenant, respect and love for Ruth, and concern for the near kinsman as he worked through the legal process to gain his wife. Certain attitudes and actions are wrong and always will be. Paul provided a long list

(II Timothy 3:2-5). The bad life centers on self and sensuality, not on God and others. Evil people manipulate and abuse the needy and weak, instead of helping them.

Chapter XV

The Family Role In Relationships

Role; the function assumed by a person. The children's role is to honor their father and mother; it suggests the idea of taking parents seriously, giving them importance in one's life and paying attention ot their place in our lives.

As a principle for effective living in the family, it has a universal quality that strengthens family relationships even among people who do not know the Lord. For believing saints, it is a direct word from God to which we must respond and for which we are accountable (Exodus 20:12). This commandment gives high regard to the mother. She is placed in a position equal to the father in receiving honor from her children (Leviticus 19:3), vows; committing someone to a prescribed role. Vows are commitments to God to perform some duty or to abstain from some activity. Instruction is given concerning an unmarried daughter living at home and a married woman living with her husband. In each case, the final authority of the male is affirmed. He has the legal responsibility for the home, and could either agree with or set aside the vow made by his daughter of wife. He had to do it as soon as he heard about it, or his silence was considered to be consent. Only if a woman was living alone as a widow or divorcee could she be the final legal authority in her own household as a woman. Men were the source of income for the household and therefore, had to give approval for any commitments made by a daughter or wife, whether or not they involved financial consideration (Numbers 30:1-15). Vows call for commitments. Jepthah's daughter knowingly agreed to her own death. Jepthah was committed to the Lord and his daughter was committed to her father and her God. A vow or promise commits a person to action before God. Jepthah made a foolish vow. Sadly his commitment was not joined with moral judgments. He should have sought God's forgiveness for a foolish vow rather than compounding the sin by sacrificing his daughter (Judges 11:30-40).

People make foolish vows that they must keep. Such as Saul made a foolish vow that his men would fast (I Samuel 14:24). Jonathan had broken that vow in ignorance of it. God considered the vow seriously and is seen in His speaking through the Lots. That the vow was itself sinful is seen in God's refusal to answer Saul and his vindication of Jonathan by giving him victory (I Samuel 14:41-45).

In Proverbs 12:4, it talks about the difference between wives who are acceptable in their behavior and those who are not. The good wife is valued as a gift from the Lord; but, the bad wife is generally a quarrelsome one. The good wife is respected by her husband and brings honor to his name

(Proverbs 18:22; 19:13-14; 21:9 and 19; 25:24; 27:15-17). Only a relationship of trust and commitment from both parties can lead to the respect and honor needed for family success. Women may play many roles in a successful family relationship. The woman is equally active in the home and business duties. She is trusted by her husband and seeks to help him at all times. She works hard, makes difficult decisions, earns and invest money well, is compassionate and helpful to the needy, is prepared for the future and has wisdom to teach others. She has earned a high reputation in her family, in the business world and in the community (Proverbs 31:10-31).

Integrity of character can be marked by our sense of purpose in life. Family responsibilities are not to be set aside to fulfill religious obligations. The Law requires faithful Jews to care for their parents in their old age, but oral tradition provided a way for selfish children to avoid this responsibility. By declaring all their property to be "corban" given to God; they could tell their parents they had no money available to help them (Matthew 15:3-6).

Jesus encourages women to use their interests and skills for spiritual growth (John 11:1-44; 12:1-3). Jesus taught and accepted to woman as one able to understand the meaning of His message; even though food is necessary to physical life, excessive attention ot housework may keep a person from experiencing even more important spiritual food. Jesus found refuge in a home even though conflicting feelings divided the family members. Jesus taught some of His most powerful truths in a family grief experience; and Jesus experienced human sorrow even though He had planned to use this experience to teach others about the power of God.

Jesus didn't limit the role of the woman (Luke 10:38-42). Paul states the concept of mutual submission to Christian family relationships; husband-wife, parent-child. In each case, self-giving of one to another is described. For the wife, it is voluntarily yielding in love to her husband's headship in the home. The husband is to yield himself to his wife in the same spirit that Jesus Christ yielded Himself to the cross to establish the Church. Children are to submit themselves to their parents in obedience, and fathers are to give themselves to the talk of guidance and discipline for their children. Mutual submission does define how individual families will determine role responsibilities in the home. It affirms a new attitude of voluntary submission in love from each family member based upon Christian faith (Ephesians 5:22-6:4).

Home relationships should honor the Lordship of Jesus Christ over the home and demonstrate to the outside world the power of the Word of God. The love shown in a Christian home should overcome non-Christians' arguments against Christianity (Titus 2:2-10). Titus strongly emphasis given to the importance of personal self-control and self-giving in order that outsiders may not be able to criticize the behavior of Christians. Men are to exemplify self-control; older women are to demonstrate reverent submission to Jesus Christ; younger women are to honor their husbands through yielding in love to their headship in the home. Peter (I Peter 3:1-7) states that Christian wives', married to non-believers, devout behavior may influence the husbands to become Christians. Christian husbands are to demonstrate their self-giving love for their wives by honoring them and showing them respect.

Chapter XVI

Family Communication In Relationships

Good communication is at the heart of good human relations. This is especially true of family relationships. There are some communication faults that cause tension in personal relationships. Honesty in speech is contrasted with using humor that hurts. Open confrontation is described as better than refusal to care enough to fact issues. Language communicates our emotions and our intellect. In so doing it attracts or repels people. Honesty and helpfulness are encouraged, whereas lying, slandering and rage are condemned. Unwholesome language grieves the Holy Spirit, who is present in the Church or home at all times.

Parents, listen to your children; listen to what they have to say. Listening is the accurate perception of what is being communicated. It is the art of separating fact from statement, innuendo and accusation. Listening is a process in perpetual motion. It begins when one hears or observes what is being said, continues as one stores and correlates the information, then begins with one's reaction. Listening is a two-way exchange in which both parties involved must always be receptive to the thoughts, ideas and emotions of others. Be open minded with your children. When you are unable to listen to your children, chances are it's because you are too busy listening to yourself. If you listen, you may be able to help your children; because what we hear isn't always the same as what's being communicated. Listen for the real truth. Train your ears to listen. Think of your home environments as the backdrop that makes your questions and problems stand out in bold relief. Listen to the particulars of that environment; your family's productivity, the goals of your family, the objectives of the home and even your listening blocks – and that will begin to train your ear on your problems and possible solutions as well.

Listening enables a person to know something of another's world. Parents, the children are watching you as an example, so "Let no corrupt communication proceed out of your mouth, but that which is good to the use of edifying, that, it may minister grace unto the hearers." (Ephesians 4:29) Be open minded with your children. Pay attention to them, be receptive, suspend judgment – set it aside for the moment. It can block or distract communications with your children. When you are speaking to your children, give them a chance to respond. In communicating with our children, we are risking a chance in losing our children. So, we need to focus on our communication process. The process of focusing involves looking at all sides of something or someone. It means fixing our gaze and trying to see more deeply into some dimension of life than we have seen before. When your children come to you with a problem, respond to them with an understanding skill, that is with the listening process. Responding with understanding gives the children the feeling that we are with them. When the things we say and do reflect that, we have heard their message and have received it non-judgmentally. The foundation for friendship has been laid. When discussing a matter with your children, don't pre-evaluate and find your opinion about them. Don't be too controllable; give your children a chance to explain themselves. Your goal, as parents, is to be an active listener and understand your children's opinion, thoughts and feelings. Your children just want you to listen to them, if not they will go to someone else. Parents don't let communication barriers stand in the way of your communication with your children.

Words have meaning. Communication can become more effective, if we recognize that "meaning" resides in people. Words are only labels pointing toward the meaning. Think before you speak and listen, so that we are able to properly interpret the information that we received. Communicate what you feel and believe. Confused language will stop the progress. Don't use false opinions and reasons from people. It will corrupt your communication with your children. When there is inconsistency between words and body language, the words say "yes" and the body language says "no." Body language is the more accurate message your children will believe what you do, not what you say you'll do. The first and most important classroom in the school of life is the home. Both father and mother are to assume responsibility for training and nurturing the minds of children. This is done by correction and effective communication. Though school and church might contribute significantly to the process of education, no outside agency can equal the influence of parents as an educative force. Parents' teaching through communication is basic to family living and to society's longer education programs. Such teaching should lead to a commitment to the Lord. Through effective communication, parental teaching helps younger adults avoid tragic mistakes. Parents must discipline children, in order for children to have a chance in life. Without discipline and correction, they will never learn. Parents should take time to communicate with their children.

Good communication is at the heart of good human relationships. This is especially true of family relationships. If the husband and wife are able to talk freely and with feelings of mutual sharing, then almost everything else can be helped. The husband and wife that are prepared to talk about whatever they want to talk about. Any topic will do because it provides an opportunity for two people to share their thoughts, feelings and emotions in a mutually appreciative way. The husband should be interested in and attentive to problems in their marriage that can be solved by thoughtful communication, and never from the top of their heads. But pay close attention to informal communication, of which are rumors, scuttlebutts and gripes. His goal is to anticipate difficulties and in this way to avoid them through effective communication. The husband's communication to promote understanding and to earn the agreement of his wife for actions to be taken, because the husband is the head of the household. Authentic communication is the basis to achieving these communication goals. What this means is that he doesn't alter the message that needs to be understood just to make it easy to swallow. Neither does he shove the message down his wife's throat. What he does is to present problems in the most honest, realistic and objective terms he is capable of. This means, he describes any given problem in terms of what the current difficulty being encountered is, what he sees to be the cause of it, and what he sees to be the on-going consequence. He may also indicate possible solutions, if he has clear cut ideas as to what a good solution might be. The husband communicates frequently with his wife. He wants to ensure himself that everything is okay in the sense that his wife is feeling good. The best way he can do this is to stay in close, chatty conversation. Then he can detect any rumblings of unhappiness, as they first begin to appear, or take time to relieve whatever tensions may exist. Never be too busy to communicate with your spouse. Be always ready to discuss whatever topic is of interest to your spouse. All of this has the possibility of creating an easy-going, giving and take kind of situation where production is neglected.

Everyone makes mistakes and errors. Husbands' or wives' attitude toward mistakes and errors are to accentuate the positive and eliminate the negative. They can do this by not blaming one another. Encourage one another with the attitude "forgiving" and "forgetting." "Harsh" attitudes toward mistakes and errors can hurt good relationships. They can produce friction, disrupt harmony, and chill the kind of warmth and harmony that the husband and wife have a right to enjoy in their interactions with one another.

The husband communicates to promote understanding and earn the agreement of his wife for actions to be taken, because the husband is the head of the household.

Authentic communication is the basis to achieving these communication goals. The right words make good communication (Titus 1:9). When communicating, use the right tone in your voice. Use watchful words, speak very frankly and use peculiar expressions when you are communicating with one another. You need to watch the way you speak, your manner and attitude of presentation. Meditate about what you are going to say. You need to watch when you speak; guard your timing. Words can hurt or heal.

Good communication is at the heart of human relationships. This is especially true of family relationships. Don't speak until you have thought about what you will say. Don't speak until you have thought about the effect of what you will say. What you say must build-up, not destroy. Even negative should be stated in an uplifting way and your motive for speaking then should be to edify one another. What you must give to those who hear should contribute to their happiness, be worth repeating and be said with the proper tone. What you say must need to be said, when you say it. It must be needful for the moment. Needful words make a positive contribution speak the truth in love. There is a right way and a wrong way to state the truth. Don't lie to your spouse; weigh the consequence. Ultimately, you will hurt yourself, if you lie. Lying is self-destructive, impermanent, brings no satisfaction, kills your joy and paralyzes you with feelings of guilt and fear; plus, it destroys trust in relationships.

Chapter XVII

Family Intermarriage

Intermarriage with followers of other religions is universally condemned in the Old Testament, because of the temptation of idolatry within the family relationship (Deuteronomy 7:3-4). This prohibition of intermarriage is not based on differences of race or culture, but on differences in religion. No marriage can be entered into with eyes closed to the possible harm of conflicting faith. Solomon followed the political pattern of his day in making political alliances through marriage. In so doing, he rebelled against God's pattern for His people. Neither political strategy nor community acceptance justifies sinful behavior. Marriages cemented political alliances for Solomon. The marriages introduced false religions to Israel. God saw them as sin (I Kings 11:1-9; Genesis 16:1-16). Imitating your father's sin does not excuse you from guilt (II Chronicles 11:18-21).

Ezra made the most direct attack on intermarriage, (Ezra 9:1-10; 17) on unbelievers in the Bible. He demanded the dissolution of marriages, which threatened to guide the rebuilding Exile community away from God. A crisis action is not meant to justify divorce, as a practice. It teaches the importance of family life to the religious well-being of God's people and shows the danger of intermarriage with unbelievers. Jewish men found the local women more attractive than the Jewish women, a latter still bore the scars of the arduous journey from Babylon to Israel. Complicating matters, the non-Jewish women generally underwent a conversion of sorts, so that their status was unclear. Jewish Law stipulates that conversion to Judaism must stem solely from a desire to become part of the Jewish people and to adhere to God and His Law. If an alternative motive such as the desire to marry a Jew is involved, the conversion lacks validity (Ezra 10:12-14). Ezra could not pass a general decree ordering the banishment of all women of non-Jewish descent, because it was possible that some of them were sincere converts. The Judges of Israel had no choice but to review each case of a mixed marriage individually, and so determine the true status of the woman. Even though the over whelming majority of Jews were not guilty of taking foreign wives, they shared some of the guilt. Ezra wisely avoided an open confrontation with those Jews who had intermarried. He was well aware that it is not a simple matter for a man to banish a beloved wife, and in some cases, also the children she bore him. In an effort to avoid open conflict and even possible violence, Ezra relied on the effect his weeping and praying would have on the people. His approach worked, for there was full cooperation from all the parties involved and the mixed marriages were broken up peacefully.

Faithfulness to family is subordinate to faithfulness to God. Nehemiah forcefully condemned the Judean men who risked their allegiance to God by marrying women who worshipped other gods (Nehemiah 10:28-30). Malachi states: "Judah has broken faith. A detestable thing has been committed in Israel and in Jerusalem. Judah has desecrated the sanctuary that the Lord loves by marrying the daughter of a foreign god (Malachi 2:11).

In verse 10, the prophet admonishes the young Israelite men for marrying non-Jewish women, or he admonishes the Israelite men for betraying their Jewish wives by marrying non-Jewish women (Ezra 10:10). Ezra says the Israelites first divorced their Jewish wives. Some say they took the non-Jewish women as second wives, but loved them more than their Jewish wives and gave them control over the household. The prophet explains why it is wrong for Israelite men to cast aside the Jewish women – they are next of kin, since all Israelites are descendants of the patriarch Jacob.

The covenant of our fathers, referring to the pact between God and the Israelites at Mount Sinai, or the verse refers to the high moral standards followed by the patriarch. Not one took additional wives without their first wives' consent (Genesis 16:2; 30:3; 30:9). By having loved and slept with; even the priests took foreign wives, or what is holy to God, that which He loved; referring to the Israelites' soul by marrying the daughter of foreign gods. Daughter of a foreign god? Foreign gods have no daughters, rather the verse teaches that whoever co-habits with a non-Jewish woman is considered, as if he had married an idol.

In the New Testament, marriage to a non-Christian is not grounds for a divorce. Such marriage provides Christian influence for the children and hope to lead the unbeliever to salvation in Jesus Christ. Such marriage is acceptable in God's sight. Divorce should not occur unless the unbelieving partner desires it (I Corinthians 7:12-16). A Christian should marry a Christian, since Christ through the Holy Spirit dwells within the believer, Christians are not to marry unbelievers and participate in their false worship. Marriage should strengthen Christian faith in God. We cannot participate in worship and practice of other religions and, or philosophies because these would dishonor God. Believers honor Jesus Christ and Him alone.

Chapter XVIII

Family Priorities

Neither military service nor business responsibilities were to take a man away from his wife during the first year of marriage. Instead, he was to remain home and bring happiness to his wife.

Giving a young marriage high priority, helps to ensure its success. "There shall not be laid upon him any public duties and responsibilities" (Deuteronomy 24:5). Jesus faced interfamily tension because of His commitment to the will of God. Even though Mary had been told that her son was destined for a particular calling in life, she, along with her other children did not understand Jesus. They feared for His mental condition and wanted to take Him home. His brothers even ridiculed Him. Jesus declared that all who would follow the will of God is His family. He did not reject His mother or family. His tender care for her at the cross indicates this (John 19:20-27). He declared that as Son of God, all who enter into close relationship with the Father become His family as well (Mark 3:31-35). Family relationships are given a high priority in the Bible, but the ultimate loyalty of every believer is to Jesus Christ as Lord. Jesus announced the potential divisions among family members that can occur because of the decision to follow, or not to follow Him (Micah 7:6). Each Christian must choose the cross. Ultimate loyalty can be given only to Jesus Christ – not to husband, wife, children or parents. Christian commitment includes faithful service to family, but Jesus Christ must be supreme (Luke 12:49-53).

In Luke 14:25-27, hate here does not refer to emotional or mental dislike of the family members mentioned nor of one's own life. Instead, it indicates a total rejection of anything and anyone who would block our absolute commitment to Jesus as Lord. The question of priority was basic in Paul's advice to widows and other unmarried persons to remain single, if they were not subject to intensive sexual desire. Paul favored singleness as a religious commitment, freeing a person to give full time to preparing people for Jesus Christ's coming. Whereas marriage placed other demands on time. Paul did not have a negative attitude towards marriage, but vocationally he believed that singleness was preferable during the crisis times ahead. He instructed younger widows to marry rather than become dependent on the Church for support

(I Timothy 5:11-14). Vocational priorities and personal gifts should determine a person's decision to marry (I Corinthians 7:8; 25-28; 32-40).

Anxiety over life is a perennial problem. Jesus' remedy for anxiety is to make the Kingdom of God and His righteousness the center of our priorities. Trusting in the trustworthy, loving, heavenly Father should replace worry, anxiety and fear in our lives. A Christian's first priority is to seek, find and follow the will of God. That is the way God's Kingdom advances. The Kingdom of God is a dynamic reality, not a static idea. It is God breaking into history to redeem and rule all who will accept responsibility for living under His rule. He is willing to give the Kingdom to all who are willing to make a covenant with Him through faith in Jesus Christ, as Savior and Lord (Matthew 6:33).

Money must not dominate life. We give the greatest thought and priority to what we really love. Jesus did not condemn money in itself. He condemned obtaining or using money instead of serving God. Anxiety over possessions is also condemned; because, it allows one to be troubled over the unknown tomorrow. God's sustaining care allows Jesus Christ's followers to follow Him without anxiety. In complete loyalty to God, love of money and anxiety over material things are attitudes which corrupt God's intended role for material possessions. These sins are caused by greed, which robs the steward of the joy and contentment of using material things to serve God (Isaiah 5:8; Micah 2:1-2). Seeking security in possessions causes much of our frustration. Only God provides true security. Secure in Him; we can meet family needs and serve others. Material needs are a reality of life that all people face. Jesus took our needs seriously and devoted much time to talking about them. Material things are not bad in themselves. They become bad when we place more importance on them than our relationship with God.

Chapter XIX

FAMILY ACCEPTING COVENANT

In the midst of a generation corrupting God's world, Noah and his family were found faithful enough to be spared the judgements of destruction by the flood. After the waters receded, God established His covenant with Noah and his family. This covenant reaffirmed the creative intent of God for humans and included a new and powerful declaration of the value of life created in the image of God.

Accepting covenant relationships with God by families is central to God's requirements throughout the Old Testament. It finds its ultimate fulfillment in the acceptance of the covenant of grace in Jesus Christ (Genesis 7:15, 22; Ephesians 5:21). Faced with the challenge of getting the land (Joshua 24:14,15), God had given to Israel, Joshua confronted the people with an unwavering choice of loyalty in their worship. The God who described Himself as a "Jealous God" (Exodus 20:5) could have no rivals in their affection. As the households in Israel, they must choose whom they would serve. In verses 16-27, the people jointed Joshua in declaring their allegiance to the covenant with the Lord and committed themselves to Him. God still desires families to make the commitment of home and shared life to Him.

Marriage to a widow of an Israelite involved intricate covenant regulations (Deuteronomy 25:7-10). Boaz showed loyalty to God's covenant respect and love for Ruth, and concern for the near Kinsman as he worked through the legal process to gain his wife (Ruth 3:1-4,12) such commitment is necessary in marriage. Family renewal was one element of God's promise to Judah. When the people would turn to Him in renewed covenant devotion. The text describes family value in Hebrew thought: absence of infant mortality, long life, secure homes, rewarding work, and many descendants. God's plan centers on family relationships on this earth (Isaiah 65:20-3).

The Abrahamic Covenant demanded circumcision of males as the seal of the covenant (Genesis 12:1-3; 17:1-18; 17:9-14). Naming the child in accord with family lineage was performed at the circumcision ceremony. The attendants were surprised when the son of Zechariah and Elizabeth was named John, rather than a family name. Mary and Joseph fulfilled the same Law of Covenant in the circumcision of Jesus (Luke 2:21). In this act, the parents accepted covenantal requirements as well as obeying the special instructions of God's revelation to each family (Luke 1:59). The Laws of the Old Testament required all male babies to be circumcised. By the time of the New Testament, all these children were circumcised either at the temple in Jerusalem or at the local Synagogue. The chief value of this action was spiritual, since it symbolized God's redemptive covenant with His people. It also was to serve as a perpetual reminder of the holy life style the individual was to maintain. Otherwise, the outward symbol would be meaningless (Leviticus 26:41). I also will walk; they will acknowledge that the calamities which had overtaken them were God's method of humbling their arrogance.

Uncircumcised; unconsecrated, unclean; closed to the divine call or appeal (Leviticus 19:23). Verse 42, Jacob . . . Isaac . . . Abraham. God is stirred to mercy by calling the noble ancestors of Israel and the covenant He entered into with each. In retrospect, the last comes first to mind.

The land; which was itself a symbol of the covenant, with the Patriarchs and prominently figured in the promises which God had made to them.

The scriptural use of the word covenant: It is used of relationships between God and man, man and man, nation and nation. It is used in things temporal and things eternal. The Abrahamic Covenant is called "eternal" in Genesis 17:7, 13, 19; I Chronicles 16:17 and Psalm 105:10). The inter-relationship of the eternal gracious covenants of God with Israel might be graphically set forth in the three aspects of the Abrahamic Covenant:

(1) The promise of a national land – Genesis 12:1; 13:14-15, 17

(2) The promise of redemption, national and universal – Genesis 12:3; 22:18; Galatians 3:16

(3) The promise of numerous descendants to form a great nation – Genesis 12:2; 13:16; 17:2-6; etc.

Therefore, it may be said that the land promises of the Abrahamic Covenant are developed in the Palestinian Covenant, the seed promises are developed in the Davidic Covenant and the blessing promises are developed in the New Covenant. This Covenant, then, determines the whole future program for the nation Israel and is a major factor in biblical Eschatology.

Chapter XX

Family Authentic Love

Ruth's fervent speech to her mother-in-law Naomi is one of the most beautiful declarations of authentic family love in the Bible (Ruth 1;15-18). It is used in wedding ceremonies to describe what marital love should be. It affirms the desire to be together, to face life's challenges together, to be a family and to worship the same God. All of these elements are essential to a healthy marriage. Marriages have laws. Ruth's statements in these two verses, 16 and 17 are in response to a particular law which Naomi had taught her as part of the conversion process:

Naomi told her, "We are forbidden to walk more than 2,000 cubits out of town

On the Sabbath."

Ruth responded, "Where-ever you go, I will go."

Naomi told her, "We are not allowed to be secluded with a member of the opposite sex."

Ruth replied, "Where-ever you lodge, I will lodge."

Naomi told her, "We are obligated in 613 commandments."

Ruth replied, "Your people are my people."

Naomi told her, "We are prohibited from worshipping idols."

Ruth replied, "Your God is my God."

Naomi told her, "The court is authorized to carry out four types of death penalties."

Ruth said, "As you die, I will die."

Naomi told her, "The executed are buried in two different burial plots; one for those

executed by stoning or burning, and one for those executed by the sword or by

strangulation.

Ruth replied, "And there I will be buried."

Song of Solomon celebrates the human love between the sexes. The Hebrew word here, defined as "love" involves the whole person in an intensity of feelings for the other, which expressed itself both in desire for that person and in self-giving to that person. The Hebrew word encompasses sexual love, friendship love and self-giving love. The marriage relationship involves all three types of love. Such love outlives death and produces a protective jealousy which allows no competition. Marital love is commitment and trust forever. It cannot be destroyed, nor can it be purchased. God gives such love to two people committed to Him and to one another.

In a world where much that looks real is not, real love in the family must be the real thing expressed in action, not merely in words. Love must be sincere; the Greek meaning authentic or undisguised. Paul gave examples of loving behavior in I Corinthians 13:4-7. Peter encouraged such love among the fellowship of faith as a demonstration of true conversion (I Peter 1:22). Love must be sincere (Romans 12:9). To do the will of God involves a disciplined application of our will in the matters of life. This begins with a goal of doing good rather than evil to other persons no matter how they treat us (Matthew 7:1-5, 12). It rests on the attitude of love and respect for others. It involves personal humility (Matthew 18:1-10). Enthusiasm for God's work fuels our will to do His will. Faithful prayer enables us to endure the dark hours of life. Then, we can share with others in need. Humility allows us to do God's will rather than center life on pride in personal achievements. Humility lets us seek to please others and live without fighting or quarreling.

God is the Father of His people because He took them in their weakness and raised them to be a mature nation. As long as they have existed, God's people have known His love. They grew up in His love. His love cured their ills and His love sought to steer them on the right track. When Israel was young, God loved her. She grew old with ingratitude and infidelity. God would have preserved Israel in the vigor of youth, but Israel rejected the election love of God. God's unconditional love merited with compassion. In His faithfulness, He could not totally give up His people (Hosea 11:1-11).

Chapter XXI

Family Parental Failure

Unwillingness to confront children when their actions are contrary to family expectations encourages them to continue those actions. David failed to exercise parental responsibility in this case (I Kings 1:6). The long range result was revolt and ultimately death for David's son. His father had never restrained him by saying, "Why are you doing this?" He never punished him. David had treated Absalom and Amon similarity, with similar result; all were headstrong and wanted to usurp the throne. Whoever fails to reprove his son is responsible for his death.

Parental discipline helps young adults avoid tragic mistakes. When parents don't discipline their children, their lives will end up in tragic mistakes such as: jail, prison, steading drugs, strong drink, pregnant or even murder. This means that the parents failed and ruined the child's life. Parents can spare their children grief later in life, if they would correct and guide them in their young years. Parenthood means devoting prime time to loving and training children, even if other good works must be left undone.

The children of two devout men, Eli and Samuel violated the faith of the home in which they grew up in by using the office of the priest for personal gain through bribery. The Bible gives us little insight into the home life of these two families, but the disobedience of the sons to the parents and God is clearly evident. Parental responsibilities can be neglected by parents, while doing important things for God in the Church and community. To be sure that family life is not usurped so drastically by other concerns, mothers and fathers are faced with making the best choices for use of their time when children are young. Many things are valuable and important, but nothing is so important as to justify neglecting children (I Samuel 2:12-17; 22-25). Religious office brings overwhelming temptation to unqualified, inept religious leaders. Having a father in a high office does not quality a son for office. Samuel's sons did not follow in his ways (I Samuel 8:3). They took bribes and refused to "ride circuit" to provide courts all over Israel.

Nothing can prevent God from punishing a wicked person when God determines to do so. Such punishment may bring sorrow and emotional suffering to others. When humans sin, especially that of religious leaders, deserves punishment. God in His way and time punishes. No leader or group of leaders is indispensable to God. If they deserve punishment because of immoral deeds, they can expect God to discipline them. Though Eli himself was a righteous man and a great leader of Israel, his sons were wicked. They filled important religious positions, but were totally inept and unqualified. Their wickedness is demonstrated in a lack of regard for priestly customs regarding their portion of the sacrifices brought to the altar. Righteous parents are no guarantee of righteous children. Spiritual office is no guarantee of spiritual leaders.

Chapter XXII

Family Violence

Jealousy among family members and the desire for power incited violent attacks upon other members of the family among the rulers in Israel and Judah (II Chronicles 21:1-8). Jehoram, son of Jehoshaphat slaughtered his brothers along with other princes of Israel to overt any threat to the throne. His sin brought God's judgement upon his family and upon himself (verses 12-20).

The King's family life does not describe that of the ordinary people in that day. Violence towards family members and sexual abuse of children were forbidden by law and were not characteristic of Hebrew families. Such examples illustrate the extreme results of the sins of jealousy, pride, and the hunger for personal power.

The murder in the Old Testament seems to major on the "what" and "how" of an incident, but do not develop the "why" of an incident beyond the matter of revenge. In a world dominated by cause and effect values, little time is given to reconciliation. Therefore, often times the murders associated with political intrigue, war and interpersonal conflict do not reflect normative, timeless principles for dealing with injustice. Caution must be applied before making quick jumps of application to contemporary time based on such incidents. Such caution asks from where the initiative comes for any acts of killing.

Cain's jealousy and anger determined his decision to kill his brother. These sinful emotions erupted when God accepted Abel's sacrifice, but did not look with favor upon Cain's. Nothing in the passage would lead to assume that Cain was in any way coerced into killing his brother. He had to bear the responsibility for his sinful jealously and anger, and for the resulting sinful act. He could not blame his parents. No matter how unjust life appears to be or how badly our ancestors handed life, we cannot lay our sin on someone else's shoulders. Each of us must bear responsibility for our own personal sinful actions (Genesis 4:6-12). Cain opened the door of his passions of envy, anger, violence, and even in murder. Passion and evil imagination are ever assaulting the heart of man; yet he can conquer them, if only he resists them with determination. Cain not only slew Abel, but also his unborn descendants. He who destroys a single human life is, as if he destroyed a whole world.

Joseph incurred the wrath of his brothers when he shared his dreams of his leadership above them (Genesis 37:1-17). His brothers hated him because of his dreams. Joseph had made himself disliked by his brothers for reporting on them; and Jacob, in giving him a coat of many colors marked him for the chiefship of the tribes at his father's death. Add to this the lad's vanity in telling his dreams, and the rage of the brethren becomes intelligible. Joseph is at first the clever child of a large family, too untutored in life to veil his superiority. His father rebuked him because his words were deepening the ill-will against him, among his brothers. His brothers were envied of him because the repetition of the dreams were a sign to them that it was more than a dream. The envisioned him his assured greatness. And now, that envy was added to hatred. They were in a mental state to do him violence. One of the hardest things to learn is to recognize without envy the superiority of a younger brother. "Behold this dreamer; master of dreams." The brothers spoke of him with bitter derision, which bodies ill for him. His brothers wanted to kill him and then throw in in a pit. Pits; cisterns, where water was stored; the opening is narrow, so that anyone imprisoned in them could not get out unassisted. I believe that Simeon wanted Joseph to be killed, but Reuben's first appear of no murder; he then hopes to outwit them by a stratagem. He appeals to them that at least they need not shed any blood; hoping later to rescue Joseph and being him back to Jacob.

They stripped Joseph of his coat; tore off with violence. They took Joseph and cast him into the pit. The pit was empty; no water in it. But it did contain serpents and scorpions. They sat down to eat bread; while the piercing cries of their doomed brother were still ringing in their ears. Nothing can more forcibly paint the callousness of all humans' feelings, which comes from slavery to hate. Judah's idea was to sell

Joseph, "Come and let us sell him to the Ishmaelites . . ." and his brothers harkened unto him, Harken unto him; the horror of their contemplated murder by starvation dawns upon them; they agree to a less violent scheme.

CHAPTER XXIII

FAMILY SYMBOLIC NATURE

Wisdom in Proverbs is intellectual, experiential and religious. Parental guidance was the inspired writer's model for the teacher student relationship. Parent teaching is basic to family living and to society's longer educational program. Such teaching should lead to commitment to the Lord, the source of all wisdom (Proverbs 1:8-9). Marital intimacy offers appropriate language to symbolize God's relationship to His people. Ezekiel 16:8-9; used the sexual union to symbolize God's establishment of covenant with Judah.

In the remainder of the Chapter, he symbolized the infidelity of Judah by using marital and family terms. In spite of her infidelity, the covenant love of God would never be totally lost. In Hosea 1:1-8; Hosea's marriage became a prophetic sign symbolizing Judah's rejection of God in favor of Baal. Marriage language was appropriate because Baal worship included sexual fertility rites. Hosea denounced the actions of the people and declared that only God could enter into a true marriage alliance with Israel. The symbolic names given to the children and the purchasing again of Gomer are designed to show both the separation of people from Yahweh, their God, and His intention to bring them back into an intimate relationship with Himself. Hosea received God's revelation during the reign of four Kings. He communicated the word with words and with his family life. God's word in this sense is the intention God wanted to reveal to his people and their leaders. Symbolizing the Church as the bride of Jesus Christ is found in Paul's writings, as well as in Revelation 21:2,9; where the New Jerusalem represents the body of believers in Christ (II Corinthians 11:2). As the bride of Christ, the Church must serve Him with sincere and pure devotion.

The Church as the bride; several New Testaments written use the marital relationship as a figure of the relationship between Christ and His Church. Most of these occurrences appear in the book of Revelation (19:7,9; 21:9; 22:17). Ephesians 5:24-33 and II Corinthians 11:1-6, also refer to the image of the Church as the bride of Jesus Christ. John, the Baptist, identified the Messiah with the bridegroom (John 3:39). The book of Revelation contains the highest conception of the Church, as the bride associated with the New Jerusalem, which comes from heaven. The imagery of the bride suggests purity and faithfulness, as well as eager longing for the wedding day. In Exodus 12:24-29; whenever the Passover meal has been observed in Jewish homes down through the centuries, its symbolism has been used to retell the story of the Exodus from Egypt.

Chapter XXVI

Family Sexual Fulfillment

Rape, the forced, sexual violation of a woman is one of the most graphic examples of the misuse of God's gift of sexuality. The consequences of Shechem's violation of Dinah brought death and destruction on the men of the City, even though Shechem wanted to marry Dinah after his sexual experience with her. Dinah's brothers justified deceit, plundering and murder because of what had happened to her. The sexual sin created destructive effect for many people unrelated to the actual sexual crime (Genesis 34:1-31).

In all ages rape is a thing that should not be done. Sexual relationships with members of both the primary and extended family were practiced by the inhabitants of the land that the Israelites were to possess. Engaging in such sexual activities is not only destructive to family relationships, but also destructive to one's relationship to God (Leviticus 18:6-20). The Bible affirms that even the land becomes polluted by such sexual misbehavior among the people. No human logic can make it right for us to go beyond God's limits in our sexual behavior. Sexual sins cannot be lightly regarded.

Hebrew faith placed great emphasis on women remaining virgins until marriage. Parents made every effort to guard daughters against premarital sexual activities. The Bible condemns sex outside marriage (I Thessalonians 4:1-6). Sexual relations are intended for marriage; women have God given rights and cannot be easily disposed of as property by ill-tempered men (Deuteronomy 22:13-28). Sexual relations outside of marriage is sin. No office or position exempts a person.

Adultery was forbidden by Hebrew Law (Exodus 20:14); (Leviticus 20:10). But David's desire for Bathsheba caused him to ignore God's Law. The web of sin enlarged to include further deceit and the planned murder of a faithful soldier. David's transgression is a classic example of the growth of sin (II Samuel 15:1-18; 18).

Sexual sin has its destructive effects, but it is not unforgiveable when repentance is real and a new commitment to God is made (II Samuel 11:2-12:13). Parental teaching helps young adults avoid tragic mistakes. Among such tragedies is the disaster of sexual sins with immoral women and wayward wives. Such sin begins with flirtatious looks and ends with disastrous punishments (Proverbs 6:20-35). An unchaste married woman has the ability to lure even a righteous person to sin, by entrapping him. Sexual sins show the destruction of a people. Only people who forget God can commit such sins (Ezekiel 22:6-11); sexual offenses against a father; they committed incest with their mother or step-mother, raped women in their impurity, one man with his friend's wife, defiled his daughter-in-law and raped his father's daughter. Actual adultery is a physical act; but the sin begins as a thought, desire, or plan in one's mind or heart. Lustfully describes an intensive and continuing desire to possess another person sexually that becomes obsessive in its control or one's mind (Matthew 5:27-30).

The seventh commandment regards the matter of adultery (Exodus 20;14); do not commit the physical act of sexual immorality; that is, remain sexually faithful to our mate for the duration of your life. One consequence of human rejection of God's plan for life is homosexual activity. The biblical revelation uniformly declares heterosexual relationships to be God's intended form of sexual interactions and condemns homosexual acts (Leviticus 18:22; 20:13). A homosexual life-style is contrary to the gospel (I Corinthians 6:9; I Timothy 1:10; Romans 1:26-28). The Church's silence encourages sexual immorality. A church member was having sexual relations with his step-mother. Whether his father was still living or whether the member was married to her is not known. Interpreters assume that the woman was not a Christian,

(I Corinthians 5:12) since Paul passed no judgment on her.

The Church must actively oppose sexual immorality, which threatens the church and family life. The Church must work to restore the repentant sinner (I Corinthians 5:1-5);

(I Timothy 1:10). All unions between the sexes that are repellent to the finer feelings of man, or would taint the natural affection between near relations are sternly prohibited. Primary prohibited marriages are: (a) blood relations – mother, sister, daughter, granddaughter, father's sister and mother's sister; (b) cases of infinity – the wives of blood relations and the wife's blood relations. All unions – whether temporary or permanent – between persons belonging to these groups are classed as incestuous. They have no binding force whatsoever in Jewish Law, and can in no circumstance be deemed a marriage. No divorce is required for their dissolution. The issue is legitimate (Leviticus 18:6-18). Secondary prohibited marriage; as the mother is forbidden, so ....

CHAPTER XXV

FAMILY DIVORCE

In Deuteronomy 24:1-4; it specifies two things concerning divorce; <u>the man</u> divorcing his wife must give her a written statement intended to protect <u>the woman</u>, and a divorced woman who remarries cannot return to her first husband, if her second husband dies or divorces her. The process of divorce was between families rather than being a legal matter at that time. If the woman was guilty of misconduct, her father would have to forfeit her dowry. If she was divorced without blame, he could demand the return of some of it. What we have here is no law instituting or commanding divorce.

This institution is taken for granted, as in Leviticus 21:7 and Numbers 30:10. It's just saying that if a man who has divorced his wife may not remarry her, if her second husband divorced her or died. Marriage is not a trade in business. This passage, Malachi 2:13-16; is the strongest statement in the Old Testament against divorce among the covenant people. Deuteronomy 24:1-4, describes a divorce process for the Hebrew people. Ezra commanded divorce from the heathen wives (Ezra 10:10-14). Malachi condemned the practice of divorcing older wives married within the covenant community to marry younger women or women of the mixed tribes who had remained in Israel during the Babylonian captivity. The Prophet anticipated the teaching of Jesus, that all divorce is contrary to God's original intention for marriage (Matthew 19:4-9). Betrothal vows were as binding as marriage; even though the couple did not live together until the wedding. In Deuteronomy 2:24, the betrothed virgin is called a wife, therefore, in accordance with Jewish legislation, which provided for divorce rather than stoning of the woman, Joseph planned to divorce Mary because of her apparent sexual unfaithfulness. His concern for her is apparent even though he thought her guilty of sexual sinfulness (Matthew 1;18, 19)

In Matthew 19:3-9, Jesus spoke to His audience with strong talk about marriage and divorce. The Jewish teachers were debating the meaning of Deuteronomy 24:1. Jesus said that the only reason God allowed Moses to make any provision for divorce was a concession to human sin. God's intention is that marriage is for a life-time, as seen in Genesis 1-2. Jesus affirmed God's intention for permanent marriage. He denied the husband's assumed right to divorce a woman for any reason. He warned husbands not to ruin a wife's reputation by divorcing her. He charged husbands with adultery, when they divorced an innocent wife and remarried. He placed guilt on a woman whose sexual sins destroyed a marriage. He limited or even prohibited divorce as part of God's will for marriage. Divorce involves missing the will of God for marriage partners.

<u>Verse 6.</u> One flesh - they are so united as to be no longer two, but one, each being a part of the other. For a man to break such a union as this, by putting away (divorce) his wife for every cause, is wrong.

<u>Verse 8.</u> Suffered – he did not direct it or suffer it in any such sense as to imply that God approved of it, or that it was right. It was a civil regulation of a civil government, suffered for a time or account of the wickedness of men, and in order to prevent the greater evils which that wickedness would otherwise have occasioned. It was a regulation as to the mode of putting away (divorce), not justify that wrong practice, but to lessen in some measure, its evils. Not so, from the beginning and in all its stages, this putting away (divorce) "for every cause" of one's wife was a violation of the will of God, as manifested in His works and His word.

Jewish law condemned a man for having sexual relations with his brother's wife (Leviticus 18:16), and for marrying the wife of his brother, (Leviticus 20:21) while the brother was still living. In addition, divorcing a wife to marry a divorced woman was looked upon with disfavor by the Rabbis. John, the Baptist, condemned Herod's for violating both of these regulations of Jewish law (Mark 6:17,18). We learn that Herod rejected his own wife to marry the wife of his brother, Philip, while he was still living. I Corinthians 7:10 and 11 states, "Marriage is designed for permanence." Divorce must not be seen as an easy option to escape problems. Christians married to one another should commit themselves to each other and to working out problems in the relationship. To do otherwise, goes against God's word.

Chapter XXVI

Family Forgiveness

Continuing expressions of forgiveness is a fundamental factor in Christian family life. Jesus described a fellow disciple rather than an actual brother in the home, but the principle of expressed forgiveness remains the same. God's judgment is promised to those who refuse to express forgiveness, even though they desire it for themselves (Luke 17:3-4).

We need to forgive other believers when they repent. How can we cultivate a forgiving attitude? By frequently going to Calvary and seeing the high price that was paid to secure our own forgiveness. It is significantly that immediately following Jesus' teaching on discipline and excommunication (Matthew 18:21-55), Matthew now includes a lengthy section on mercy and the need for continuous forgiveness. Peter asked a most practical question, in light of Jesus' previous discussion on disciplining your brother in the faith. Suppose your brother sin against you, repents of his wrongs, and then repeats the process a half dozen times? When do you draw the line? When do you say, "enough is enough?"

Jesus' answer was not seven times seven, but seventy-seven times in a day. How often should you forgive a sinning and repenting fellow believer (Luke 17:3-4)? Jesus sets no boundaries on forgiveness. Forgiveness is always available for those who repent. This is the way God forgives us, and it must be the way we forgive others. Jesus says if your brother sins, rebuke him; and if he repents, forgive him (Luke 17:3).

Forgiveness is not something that God gives to everyone without qualification. He makes forgiveness available to everyone and upon the individual's repentance, He instantly bestows this grace. But if there is no repentance, there can be no forgiveness. We cannot forgive someone when God, Himself has not yet forgiven them. But at the first trace of repentance, our hearts must open wide so that the flow of forgiveness will be both free and abundant.

In Jesus' teaching on the Lord's prayer, this petition is astonishing. If it consisted only of the first phrase, "and forgive us our trespasses", it might have been included, implicitly in the first three petitions of the Lord's Prayer, since Jesus Christ's sacrifice is "that sins may be forgiven." But, according to the second phrase, our petition will not be heard unless we have first met a strict requirement. Our petition looks to the future, but our response must come first, for the two parts are joined by the single word "as." And forgive us our trespasses . . .

Forgiveness; this word (in its various forms) is one of the most significant and practical terms found in the entire Bible. From Genesis to Revelation, it appears nearly 120 times. It is found in twenty-three of the Bible's books. And, appropriately enough it is located more often in the Gospels than anywhere else (forty-four times).

Here is a classic passage which unfortunately, has been the object of much misunderstanding. These words appear to be self-explanatory and self-sufficient. But here in lies the root of the problem, these verses in order to be properly understood, need to be seen in the light of a passage from Luke, namely chapter 17; verse 13. Jesus teaches the way to reclaim an offending brother; is for some brother to go and converse with him alone. If this is not effectual, he is to take one or two more witnesses and converse with him again. If that is not effectual, then it is their duty to communicate what has been done to the Church. If under their discipline he will not reform, he is to be cut off.

However numerous or aggravated are the offenses of any brother, if he give evidence of penitence by confessing and forsaking his sins, all are bound to forgive him. If we do not forgive others, God will not forgive us. An unforgiving spirit is \the spirit of perdition.

Chapter XXVII

Family New Selfhood

Jesus Christ's death demonstrated God's love for human beings who reject God's will and become enemies of grace. When we accept that love, we experience reconciliation with God. New selfhood begins (Ephesians 4:22-24). Ephesians 4:22-24 speaks of a new self. The teachings of Paul; to put off, to remove, as one puts off clothes; to put it off for once and for all; definite, concluding action; the stripping off is to be done at once, and for good. The whole character representing the former self was not only corrupt, but ever growing more and more corrupt. This is indicated by the present tense.

Every trait of the man's behavior is putrid, crumbling or inflated, like rotting waste or cadavers, stinking, ripe for being disposed of and forgotten. Verse 23: to make new again, to renew. The present tense emphasizes the continuing of renewing. To put on holiness; as in the sense of putting on a garment. It indicates fulfilling the divine demands which God places upon men. Galatians 3:26-29; the baptize; the baptism was the sign of an entry into a new kind of life. To put on; just as a garment which one puts on envelopes this person wearing it and identifies his appearance in his life. So the person baptized in Jesus Christ is entirely taken up in Jesus Christ and in the salvation brought by Him.

Romans 6:3-6; to be raised, to rise. Freshness, newness, in a new state, which is life; which becomes a change to walk, to walk about, to conduct one's life. One must be buried through baptism into death, not literally but spiritually. Just as Jesus Christ was raised from the dead, so the new Christian must be raised to live a new life. This is the primary reason for preserving the original New Testament form of baptism; immersion under water. Burial and resurrection of the Christian believer in immersed baptism bears witness to Jesus Christ's death, and resurrection declares the believer's death to an old sinful nature and resurrection to a new life.

The gospel of grace brings both men and women into a new relationship with God, self and other people. The gospel creates a new equality between men and women based upon the new selfhood in Jesus Christ. This is a spiritual equality that provides a foundation for the man and the woman to relate to each other in the home and society on a more equal basis. Jesus Christ brought a new identity to believers, joining them in His body and obliterating concern for differences which previously separated them (Galatians 3:26-29). To become new, one must put off the old self and then put on the new self (Colossians 3:5 – "Mortify therefore your members which are upon the earth.") "Mortify" in this case means "subdue." Evil desires are subdued or suppressed by means of prayer and fasting. Fasting was recommended both by Jews and Christians for the purpose of weakening the earthly desires of the body.

<u>Mortify</u>; since you are dead with Christ, act consistently in putting to death your members which are upon the earth; your bodily members as the instruments of earthly lusts; in other words, the sinful passions that exert their power in your bodily members, so that from being servants to uncleanness and to iniquity, they may become servants to righteousness (Romans 6:19).

<u>The old man</u>; those inclinations and habits which belong to man before conversion;

<u>put on</u>; adopted new principles and entered a new course of life, in consequence of having been renewed in the spirit of their minds by the Holy Ghost.

Chapter XXVIII

Family Mutual Respect

To honor one another is to show respect for the other's personhood. Such respect is essential to Christian home relationships, as well as, to life in the Church. Husbands are to treat their wives with respect (I Peter 3:7). Wives are to respect their husbands (Ephesians 5:33). Children are to respect their parents (Ephesians 6:1-6); and parents are to discipline children while still showing respect and sensitivity for the child's emotional and spiritual needs (Ephesians 6:4).

<u>In honor preferring one another</u>; rather, going before, or setting an example to one another in courtesy, kindness and respect.

<u>Giving honor</u>; due respect, kind attention, and affectional assistance; such as love guided by wisdom.

<u>Dictate, heirs together</u>; mutual partakers of divine grace, equality entitled to the blessings of the gospel (I Peter 3:7).

Each person must respect his mother and father (Leviticus 19:3), and show respect for the elderly (Leviticus 19:32). A kind hearted woman gains respect (Proverbs 11:16). God, as Father, calls forth an image of love, concern and helpfulness in our minds. It must also call us to respect, honor and serve Him (Malachi 1:6).

Paul appealed to two motivations for the Thessalonians to live up to high ethical standards. One was to please God; the other was to live so as to win the respect of those outside of the gospel. If persons knew only these two guidelines, it would be enough for them to begin and continue the journey of growing toward mature Christian character. The Christian call is always to improve on what we are already doing (I Thessalonians 4:12). Know them; as your ministers, with affectional love and obedience to their instructions (I Thessalonians 5:12).

Timothy states concerning the husbands; he must manage his own family well and see that his children obey him with proper respect (I Timothy 3:4). Honor all men by showing them proper respect (I Peter 2:17). Fear God in such a manner, as shall lead you to obey Him. All fear; all proper respect, the forward; wicked; peevish, morose.

Leviticus 19:32 states; rise up before the hoary head, "Hoary, white with age. The ethical sublimity of this exhortation is not diminished by the fact that parallels exist among other ancient people, and that in the orient, reverence for old age is or was the rule until this present day. Honor the face of the old man. Fundamental moral laws; the first precept stressed is reverence for parents. Neglect of filial duty vitiates a man's whole attitude to life, and places the idea of holiness out of his reach. If we have failed in our duty towards our parents, we are not likely to succeed in our relations towards others. Fear . . . his mother; stand in awe of . . . his mother. In the Decalogue, the father is mentioned before the mother and the word used is honor instead of fear.

Chapter XXIX

Family Needs Fulfillment

The husband and wife share mutual responsibility for the sexual fulfillment of the marriage partnership. Christians cannot claim private possession of their own bodies since in the one flesh relationship, husband and wife belong to each other. This is a distinct advance over the older concept of the wife as property, rather than a partner or the wife as only satisfying the husband's needs.

Sexual needs are a part of human nature created by God. The marriage relationship is the only relationship in which the sexual need can be truly satisfied (I Corinthians 7:2-7). For the husband and wife, sexual relationship is an obligation involved in the marital union. The marriage partners should have regular relations with one another. If not, Satan will tempt you; to try to cause you to fall. Due benevolence; these words express the mutual duty of the husband and wife toward each other. Not power of her own body; not to live apart, even for a time, without mutual consent. Defraud ye not one the other; deprive not one another by separation, of any safeguard against temptation. Do nothing which shall tend to impurity, or give Satan advantage over you. The word defraud means to deprive; deny of their need. Do not deprive husband or wife of their sexual need, except when both of you consent to do so, especially at the time when you devote yourselves to fasting and prayer; and then come together again so that Satan may not tempt you because of your physical passion. If the need is not met, it is a possibility that husband or wife could fall in sin.

Verse 9 – to burn; be disturbed with ungratified passion, or tempted by it to the commission of sin.

Proverbs 18:22 states; He (man) who finds a wife . . . He was found good because his wife will help him with his work, and he has won the favor of God because she will keep him from sinning.

II Th4ssaonians 3:10 states; "If any would not work, neither should he eat." Work is honorable and necessary. Honest industry serves both human needs and the ministries of Jesus Christ. Work is not a punishment for our sin. Sin does cause labor to be toilsome, often a struggle against circumstances (Genesis 3). Labor is an essential part of God's world. To work is to be a steward of God's world. If he does work, he should not be supported from the earnings of others. Idleness is a great sin, and the supporting of the persons by private or public, charity or in any way which encourages them in idleness should be conscientiously avoided.

Chapter XXX

Family Social Concern

Christian servanthood expresses itself in concern for the welfare of others and can be demonstrated by families. Paul encouraged Christians to pursue the grace of hospitality, a quality of caring which families can practice through their homes (Romans 12:13).

Distributing to the necessity of saints; supplying their wants. Given to hospitality; accustomed to provide for needy travelers and strangers, especially such as are laboring or suffering for Christ. God's social order is set up to prevent want and need among His people. Full obedience by His people should lead to divine blessings which would eliminate poverty. People who do not fully obey cannot demand or expect such blessings (Deuteronomy 15:5-6).

The Law of God provides a stable and durable social order. Where love, justice, honesty and reverence are woven into the fabric of society through the teaching of God's word, the people will know how to live in right relationships with God and with one another. Otherwise, widespread ignorance of the will of God provides a fertile seedbed for injustice, crime and social chaos.

In Psalm 78:1-8, the Psalmist prayed that the commandments and actions of the Lord would be studied and communicated to the next generation in the home. Only in that way can children be led to put their trust in the Lord and obey His teachings. Each individual must learn ot love and obey God. No other institution can be more effective than the home.

Human life is inherently social and needs human relationships for satisfactory development. Marriage is the fundamental response to this need; but more generally, human beings need interaction with other people to become whole persons. The larger family context of parents, brothers and sisters, spouse, children, and in-laws is the basic social unit within which personality development takes place. God's people make up the family of believers or the household of faith (Galatians 6:9-10). As God's family, the Church cares for one another in all personal needs. as well as doing what is right and good for non-believers.

In keeping with the social nature of man, the good of each individual is necessarily related to the common good, which in turn, can be defined only in reference to the human person. Do not live entirely isolated, having retreated into yourselves, as if you were already justified, but rather instead to seek the common good together. By common good is to be understood.

The sum total of social conditions which allow people either as groups or as individuals to reach their fulfillment more fully and more easily. The common good concerns the life of all. It calls for prudence from each and even more from those who exercise the office of authority. The common good presupposes respect for the person as such. In the name of the common good, public authorities are bound to respect the fundamental and inalienable rights of the human person. Society should permit each of its members to fulfill his vocation. The common good resides in the conditions for the exercise of the natural freedoms indispensable for the development of the human vocation; such as, the right to act according to a sound norm of conscience and to safe guard . . . privacy, and rightful freedom also in matters of religion.

Also, the common good requires the social well-being and development of the group itself. Development is the epitome of all social duties. It is the proper function of authority to arbitrate, in the name of the common good, between various particular interests; but is should make accessible to each what is needed to lead a truly human life; food, clothing, health, work, education and culture, suitable information and the right to establish a family. Most important, the common good requires peace, that is, the stability and security of just order. It presupposes that authority should ensure, by morally acceptable means, the security of society and its members. It is the basis of the right to legitimate personal and collective defense.

Chapter XXXI

Family Single

Jesus honored celibacy as a valid life choice, just as He honored marriage. A Eunuch is a person physically incapable of sexual union. According to Jewish Law, such a Eunuch could not be validly married. Eunuch means both "faithful and a Eunuch." This is because a Eunuch is a faithful servant entrusted with important duties. Jesus spoke of men who were born Eunuchs, those who were made Eunuchs for the Kingdom of heaven's sake (Matthew 19:12). The Minister of Finance of the Queen of Ethiopia was a Eunuch. "And he was met by a Eunuch who had come from Ethiopia (Acts 8:27).

Thousands of men left their homes, inflicted injuries upon their bodies, and sought dwelling in deserts and caves. Paul does not object to marriage; "I have no command from God" means it is not written in the Law. If circumstances should require that men should remain unmarried, let them be so. But marriage is holy and ordained by God (I Corinthians 7:28). Jesus also affirmed those who remain single by choice to fulfill a vocational commitment to service for God. Jesus' own life illustrates this commitment, as does the life of Paul (I Corinthians 7:1, 7-9).

The daughters of Philip were also unmarried by religious commitment (Acts 21:8-9). Some men and women have turned aside the pleasures of a family life. They have abhorred domestic interests because of a special burden and love for their Lord's work. Such persons are gifted of God to perform this role of single adulthood. Since Hebrew faith, the Bible does not deal explicitly with singleness as a lifestyle. It does offer guidelines to human wholeness that are applicable to singles, as well as to married persons.

Remaining single offers extra time for special service to God. It was Paul's choice of lifestyle based on a God given gift to live. The single person must be able to avoid temptations to sexual immorality.

Acts 21:9 – "And the same man had four daughters, virgins, which did prophesy." Virgins, in this case means maidens that are unmarried women. The four maidens might have been too young to be married, but Philip was an evangelist; his daughters may have been engaged in teaching and preaching, and may have had the gift of prophesying. They taught and warned people of forthcoming events.

Marriage is a common union in our world, but chastity, for the sake of God's Kingdom, is an equally acceptable state.

Chapter XXXII

Family Prayer

Paul expected married couples to pray together. I Peter 3:7, implies that prayers of a husband and wife is important. Daily family prayers are one of the most powerful means of grace; and husbands and wives should so live that uniting in it will be delightful, and a means of fitting them for the joys of earth and the bliss of heaven. The whole family should come together and pray.

In Matthew 6:6-15, Jesus teaches His disciples how to pray. After specifying the wrong way to pray, Jesus proceeds to give a sample of the right way to pray. Every necessary element for a richly spiritual life is contained in these few words. First, as ought to be expected, God and His kingdom are given the initial place in the prayer. Second, our own needs – both physical and spiritual – are mentioned in the spirit of expectancy (observe that Jesus Christ's disciples do not hoard things – "daily bread"). Third, our relationship to people is covered with the grace of forgiveness. Finally, in the fourth position, the desire for protection from satanic forces is confidently expected.

In the act of creation, God calls every being from nothingness into existence. Crowned with glory and honor, man is after the angels, capable of acknowledging how majestic is the Name of the Lord in all the earth. Man may forget his creator, or hide far from His face. He may run after idols or accuse the deity of having abandoned him; yet the living and true God tirelessly calls each person to that mysterious encounter known as prayer. In prayer, the faithful God's initiative of love always comes first; our own first step is always a response. As God gradually reveals Himself and reveals man to himself, prayer appears as a reciprocal call.

What is prayer? Prayer is the raising of one's mind and heart to God or the requesting of good things from God. We must pray out of the depth of a humble and contrite heart. He who humbles himself will be exalted. Humility is the foundation of prayer. Only when we humbly acknowledge that we do not know how to pray as we ought, are we ready to receive freely the gift of prayer. In John 4:10; it states if you knew the gift of God . . . The wonder of prayer is revealed beside the well where we come seeking water. There, Jesus Christ comes to meet every human being. It is He who first seeks us and asks us for a drink. Jesus thirsts; His asking arises from the depths of God's desire for us. Whether we realize it or not, prayer is the encounter of God's thirst with ours. God thirsts, that we may thirst for Him. When we pray it must be from the heart. According to the scripture, it is the heart that prays.

The heart is our hidden center, beyond the grasp of our reason and of others. Only the Spirit of God can fathom the human heart and know it fully. The heart is the place of decision, deeper than our psychic drives. It is the place of truth – where we choose life or death. It is the place of encounter, because as the image of God, we live in relation. It is the place of covenant. Christian prayer is a covenant relationship between God and man in Jesus Christ. It is the action of God and of men, springing forth from both the Holy Spirit and ourselves, wholly directed to God the Father, in union with the human will of the Son of God, made man. In the New Covenant, prayer is the living relationship of the children of God, with their father, who is good beyond measure with His son Jesus Christ and with the Holy Spirit,

Chapter XXXIII

Family Economic Support

Paul gave insight into his understanding of parental responsibility for children as he reminded the Corinthians of his deep care for them. Parents are to provide for their children. Adult children do have personal financial responsibility for aged parents (I Timothy 5:4, 8, 16). Economic support is still a primary function of the family, even though governmental support systems are often necessary and can be used legitimately.

In many parts of the near East, where orphan asylums and homes for old people are unknown, widows and orphans are cared for by relatives, friends and churches. The Mohammedans give a tithe for this purpose. The money is administered by the Mosque. The poor receive bread, clothing and shelter. The Jews also take care of their widows and orphans. Their concern for one another is great; their racial ties are probably stronger than those of other races. That is why one seldom sees a Jewish beggar. The scriptures make a strong plea on behalf of orphans, widows and the destitute. "He doth execute the judgement of the fatherless and widows, and loveth the stranger in giving him food and raiment. Love ye therefore the stranger; For ye were strangers in the land of Egypt." (Deuteronomy 10:18, 19) "A father of the fatherless, and a judge of the widows, is God in His holy habitation." (Psalm 68:5) Indeed, even though at times widows were treated unjustly, they were for the most part generously supported by the rich and the pious. Many women, after the death of their husband, could not earn a livelihood. The relied on support upon their relatives or the pious.

Paul warns against such practices. Not because he was against Eastern hospitality, but because there were many persons who took advantage of the generosity of pious men and women. Some widows, instead of receiving aid from their relatives, caused a burden on the people. Many women after the death of their husbands could not earn a livelihood. They relied for support upon their relatives or the pious. Such cases are so numerous that it is difficult to know which are worthy.

Easterners hated to turn away anyone who is in need. Grown children's responsibility to their parents, as much as they can, must give them material and moral support in old age and in times of illness, loneliness and distress. Jesus calls this, duty of gratitude. I Peter 5:1-5; speaks concerning supporting the Church. The care of the Church has been entrusted to those who are designated by different terms – elders, overseers (Bishops) and pastors – but who all have the same function. Peter addressed the leaders as elders, but used the imagery of shepherding (pastor) and overseeing (Bishop) to portray their responsibilities. The most prevalent term used today for this office is pastor.

The flock has been committed to the pastor who serves under the chief shepherd. Pastors are not hirelings who care nothing for the sheep. They are to tend to the flock assigned to them out of devotion to God, not to gratify their personal ambitions. They are not to serve for personal gain, whether it be for financial reward, popular acclaim or reputation. They are not to be domineering or authoritarian in their leadership. Their ministry is to be characterized by selfless serve and humility, no arrogance.

God depiones the sin of turning away from His decrees. Levitical Law required the people of Israel to give ten percent of their agricultural products plus various sacrifices and services to God (Malachi 3:10). Man's freedom; the exercise of freedom does not imply a right to say or do anything. It is false to maintain that man, the subject of his freedom, is an individual who is fully self-sufficient and whose finality is the satisfaction of his own interests in the enjoyment of earthly goods. Moreover, the economic, social, political and cultural conditions that are needed for a just exercise of freedom are too often disregarded or violated.

Chapter XXXIV

Family Accepted Grace

Through acceptance of God's grace offered through Jesus Christ, family members enter into the household of God with Jesus Christ, as the cornerstone. Paul continually affirmed the Lordship of Jesus Christ, as the foundation upon which the home is built (Ephesians 2:8-10, 19, 20).

Christians are saved by grace; you're being saved by grace through faith, all that is good in man, and all the good which he enjoys are the gracious gifts of God. It is a gift; all we have to do is receive it. "For we are his workmanship; of our spiritual life, God is the author." Before ordained; it was ever the purpose and will of God, that those to whom he gives spiritual life should be holy and abound in good works.

Grace and faith are God's gifts in Jesus Christ. We cannot exercise faith and then receive by grace God's salvation, except God's mighty work through the Holy Spirit in our lives. That is why God's grace in salvation is often called "free grace." It all comes from God and His effectual call to salvation. Jesus' saving actions created new life for believers, a life of good works. God created the elect to continue the good works of Jesus Christ. This workmanship of God has no afterthought, but a part of the predestined purpose of God. God's people are His new creation. God has redeemed His people and equipped us to do good works. Christians are not saved by good deeds, but they are saved for God to do good deeds through them.

God's presence became a human being and revealed the fullness of God's identity in flesh. The glory of God (Exodus 33:22), became visible as grace and truth, which all people need. He is a greater revelation than Moses' Law, which revealed God's guidelines for life. He showed that those guidelines can really be lived out in human flesh on earth. He is God in flesh, letting us see what otherwise was impossible to see (John 1:17).

The Law was given to Moses; a certain measure of grace accompanied the Law of Moses, else no man could have been saved under it. Yet the proper office of the Law itself was not grace, but rather restraint and conviction of sin (Romans 3:20; Galatians 3:19). Grace and truth came by Jesus Christ. All the grace that belonged to the dispensation of the Law came through Jesus Christ. While the gospel, which He revealed, is itself grace and truth in full measure. The grace of Jesus Christ is not in the slightest way a rival of our freedom when this freedom accords with the sense of the true and the good that God has put in the human heart. As a Christian experiences tests, especially in prayer, the more docile we are to the promptings of grace, the more we grow in inner freedom and confidence during trials, such as those we face in the pressures and constraints of the outer world.

By the working of grace, the Holy Spirit educates us in spiritual freedom in order to make us free collaborators in His work in the Church and in the world. Paul states; "I besought the Lord thrice"; the answer was; "My grace is sufficient"; to enable you with patience to bear it, support and comfort you under it, and make you more happy and useful than you would be without it (II Corinthians 12:9).

Chapter XXXV

Family Continuing Growth

Paul prayed for the disciples to grow in love, knowledge, insight and fruitfulness (I Corinthians 13:11-12; Ephesians 4:14-15; Colossians 1:9-12). Since the family and church are described in similar terms, family members also are to grow in all of these needs, as they give respect and honor to each. Spiritual growth is essential for the Christian family.

Ephesians speaks of a child; a man; as the conceptions and speaks of a lisping infant differ from these of an educated and full-grown man, so do our highest attainments in this life differ from what they will be in the life to come. Childish things; the imperfect conceptions and reasoning of a child. Supply; so in heaven we shall put away our imperfect conceptions of God's truth, and our imperfect helps for gaining it. Now; in our present earthly state. We see through a glass, darkly; our knowledge of God and divine truth is indirect and obscure, like that of a man who looks not directly on the object itself, but only on a divine image of it. Such as was reflected from the imperfect mirrors of the accents. But then; in the heavenly state. Speaking truth; by walking in truth, being truthful in word and deed. May grow up into him; so as to become mature men in him. In all things; in all parts of our Christian character. Hebrews states, leave the principles of the doctrine of Christ. Principles; elements or first rudiments of religion. Unto perfection; maturity in the knowledge and obedience of the Gospel (verse 1; verse 4). Enlightened; in the knowledge of the gospel of the Gospel. II Peter 3:18 states, "Grow in grace, increase your knowledge of Christ and your likeness to him."

Paul states in Ephesians 4:13-15; till we all come; come fully. In the unity of the faith and of the knowledge of the Son of God; better, as the margin into the unity, etc.; meaning that unity which full establishment in the faith and knowledge of the Son of God gives. For the greater the measure of our faith and knowledge, the greater our unit in that faith and knowledge, and thus our unity with God and each other. Unto a perfect man; a full-grown mature man, in contrast with babes in Christ. Verse 14-the fullness of Christ; the fullness that belongs to Christ; that is, Christ considered in His body the Church. Verse 15-speaking the truth; the original word means rather, walking in the truth, being truthful in word and deeds. May grow up into him; so as to become mature men in Him. Verse 13-I'm all things; in all parts of our Christian character.

Peter states in II Peter 3:18, "Grow in grace, and in the knowledge of our Lord and Savior Jesus Christ." This is the unfailing panacea for all spiritual ills. As we go on to know

Christ better and become increasingly like Him, and as we are freed upon His word and it has its way over our hearts, our progress will be consistent and continuous. God's people ought to be spotless and blameless, guarded and growing in view of the events of the end times. Since God is holy, to be Godlike is to be holy. To be holy is to be distinct from the ordinary and worldly.

Moral blamelessness must be maintained. The influence of error and evil demands persons who are on guard, the prospect of meeting the Lord, encourages growth the in grace and knowledge of Jesus Christ. The sincere expectations of the Lord's coming promotes personal purity. We are to grow by the preaching of the gospel of Jesus Christ; I have planted. Paul first preached the gospel to the Corinthians and gathered the Church. Apollos watered; he came after Paul and further instructed the people. God gave the increase; all the success of both was from God (I Corinthians 3:6).

Chapter XXXVI

Family Creation

Marriage is part of God's purpose in creation and should not be forbidden (I Timothy 4:3-5). Material things are not by nature evil; neither the healthy sexual relationships of marriage nor certain foods are sinful in themselves. God ordained marriage and procreation at creation (Genesis 1:28; 2:24,25). Everything He created was "very good." (Genesis 1:26). We are to use the personal relationships and material things God gives us, thanking Him for them and dedicating them to His purposes. I repeat every creature; which God hath made for food is good for food, and not to be abstained from, but to be eaten with gratitude to God the giver. For it is sanctified; made holy to him who partakes of it, so that the use of it cannot defile him. By the word of God; ordaining it for man's use. Prayer; which procures from God a blessing upon it. (Genesis 1:31). Very good; each created thing is good in itself; but when combined and united, the totality is proclaimed very good.

Everything in the universe was as the Creator willed it. Nothing superfluous, nothing lacking – a harmony. This

131

harmony bears witness to the unity of God who planned this unity of nature. Though nature seems to be indifferent to man's sense of compassion. The world is good, since goodness is its final aim; without struggle, there would be no natural selection or adaptation to changing surroundings, and therefore, no progress from lower to higher. And God saw everything that He had made, and behold, it was very good – evil in suffering, evil, nay death itself, have a rightful and beneficent place in the divine scheme.

False teachers trouble the Church with false rules. God's rules are good for us and bring joy and thanksgiving into our lives. A key to determining if an action is right, is its ability to make us praise and thank God. Holiness does not depend on legal specifications, but on relationship with God and in prayerful fellowship with God gratefully acknowledging Him. As an invariable source, Christians hollow everything we touch.

Forbidding to marry; as puberty forbids the clergy, and endorses monks and nuns to take vows of celibacy, declaring, as did the Council of Trent, "Whosoever shall say that the married state is to be preferred to a state of virginity or celibacy, let him be accursed." Commanding to abstain from meat; as puberty does during Lent, on fast day, and days abstinence. To received; for food, and eaten by believers who know the will of God, during Lent, as well as at other times. Every creature; which God hath made for food is good for food, and not to be abstained from, but to be eaten with gratitude to God the giver. Sanctified; made holy to Him who partakes of it, so that the use of it cannot defile him. By the word of God; ordaining it for man's use. Prayer; which procures from God a blessing upon it,

"In the beginning God created the heavens and the earth." (Genesis 1:1) Three things are affirmed in these first words of scripture: (1) the eternal God gave a beginning to all that exists outside of Himself; (2) He alone is Creator and (3) the totally of what exists depends on the one who gives it being. "In the beginning was the word … the word was God … all things were made through Him, and without Him was not anything made that was made." (John 1:1) The New Testament reveals that God created everything by the eternal word, His beloved Son. In Him all things were created, in heaven and on earth … all things were created through Him and for Him. He is before all things, and in Him all things hold together. The Church's faith likewise confesses the creative action of the Holy Spirit, the giver of life. "The Creator Spirit, the source of every good." The Old Testament suggests that the New Covenant reveals the creative action of the Son and Spirit inseparably one with that of the Father. This creative cooperation is clearly affirmed in the Church's rule of faith; "There exists but one God … He is the Father, God, the Creator, the Author, the Giver of order. He made all things by Himself, that is by His word and by His wisdom", by the "Son and the Spirit." Who, so to speak are "His hands." Creation is the common work of the Holy Trinity.

Chapter XXXVII

Family Special Concerns

Family Bible Study

Faithful Jews in Israel were required to read the Torah twice daily to remind them of their faith in one God and their dependence on His word. The central theme of having God's commandments in the heart and teaching them in the home is as relevant to modern Christian home, as it was to Jewish homes n the biblical world (Deuteronomy 6:4-9). Reading and talking about the word of God is intended to be normal part of everyday life in the home rather than some formal time that is distinct from other home activities.

Parents should share their own faith in God in times of crisis and joy to influence children to understand the reality of God's presence. Families reading the Bible together in response to questions and problems will help make it real for life in the minds of parents and children alike. After the repetition of the story of the giving of the Ten Commandments, Moses proceeds to declare the other great foundation of the Torah; the oneness of God and Israel's undivided loyalty to Him. Here the foundational truth of the unity of God is proclaimed. It is followed by the fundamental duty founded upon that truth. The devotion to Him of the Israelites whole being. He is bidden to love God with heart, soul and might; to remember all the commandments and instruct his children in it; to recite the words of God when retiring or rising; to bind those words on the arm and head, and to inscribe them on his door posts and the city gates.

Family Shared Joy

Joy is a distinctive quality of biblical faith in both the Old Testament and New Testament. In this verse, Jesus found joy in the disciples. He prayed their joy might overflow in abundance because of their relationship to Him and to each other. Joy is intended to be shared whether in worship or family togetherness (Deuteronomy 16:14-15).

The Christian family amplifies joy because a relationship with Jesus Christ guides family relationships. Uniting the family in Christian faith results in joy for the family (Acts 16:34). Good family relationships bring joy (Proverbs 10:1; 15; 20). Happy experiences can be shared in joy (Luke 1:58). Times of difficulty bring grief, but grief can be turned into joy, such as the joy of having a child overcomes the pain of childbirth (John 16:20-22). Joy is a gift of God (Acts 14:17). Shared family experiences of joy create memories that continue through life. Families need to guard against letting the difficulties of daily tasks rob them of time to plan enjoyable experiences together (John 15:11). Joy is mentioned here as a spiritual fruit, as well as in the familiar quotation of Galatians 5:22. A wise son spends his days in the study learning the love of God alongside his father, who derives great joy from hearing his son's wise words. But a foolish son spends much of his time loafing at home in the presence of his mother, which saddens her to no end (Proverbs 10:1).

Often, the Bible defines salvation as joy. Joy is the direct response one has to salvation. God's joy is greater than the abundance of food and drink. Such joy leads us to spontaneous praise of God (Psalms 4:7). Every family needs joy in their home. Any good, real, substantial happiness; put gladness in my heart; through loving, trusting in, and obeying you while you lifest upon me the light of Thy countenance. Satisfying enjoyment can be found only in doing the will of God, and in His love.

Family Rejecting Parents

Parents symbolically represent God to the children. Therefore, rejecting parents is not only disobedience to them, but also rejects God's established order for family life. When a son consistently rejected parental discipline and lived a life contrary to God's will for Israel, the Law prescribed the death penalty (Exodus 21:15, 17; Leviticus 20:9). The penalty was on the sin of disobedience to God as much as rejection of parents (Deuteronomy 21:18-20).

Exodus 21:15; "Anyone who attacks his father or mother must be put to death." A disobedient son; Israel parents were particularly affectionate and even indulgent. However, an incorruptible son whom milder measures failed to reclaim, might be tried by the elders at the gate, and was liable to death by stoning. A son that is stubborn and rebellious; a son who throws off the authority of his parents, as well as of God.

Crimes Against Parents

"And he that smiteth his father or mother shall be surely put to death; smiteth his father or mother shall be surely put to death. Smiteth; the rule that only when the blow left. A bruise was the death penalty incurred.

Family God's Judgement

Judgement comes upon families when fathers lead the family into idolatry. Idolatry is the extreme admiration, love or reverence for something or someone more than God. The Old Testament prophets described in graphic terms God's judgement upon the nation, including families when the people followed false gods instead of remaining faithful to their covenant with Him (Jeremiah 913-16).

Prayer becomes useless for families who forget they made a covenant to obey God and who ignore the lessons of judgement from history. Faithfulness to the one God is the first lesson of history. When families conspire together to deceive God and His people, they bring God's judgement on the individual in the family (Acts 5:1-11). Being privy; secretly knowing and concurring in the design of keeping back a part of the price for which they sold the land, while they professed to bring the whole. The Holy Ghost; who was present with the Apostles and under whose direction they acted. While it remained; before he sold it. In thine own power; at his disposal. It was optional with him to give it to the Apostles or not; as he chose. There was no constraint or compulsion in this matter, but it was entirely voluntary. Unto God; by lying to the Holy Ghost, who was with the Apostles, they lied unto God; for He was God. Gave up the Ghost; instantly died (Acts 5:1-11).

Family Temporal

Jesus affirmed marital relationships as we know them to be for this life only (Mark 12:18, 27; Luke 20:27-38). The Sadducees wanted Jesus to tell them who a woman will be married to in heaven if she had more than one husband on earth. Jesus told them that, "There will be no marriages in heaven." (Matthew 22:23-33) Individuals experience life after death, but the Bible does not give specific instructions on the nature of personal interaction in heaven by those who have been married on earth.

The Bible is the textbook of the Christian faith. The Old Testament sheds light on the mission and teachings of Jesus Christ; and the New Testament enlarges our understanding of the message of Israel's prophets. Christian teaching must be based on scriptures, must point to Jesus Christ and must not contradict scripture. As we study the recorded teachings of Jesus, the Spirit gives insight into their meanings. The Spirit is present at the Christian's study desk and in every Christian study group leading believers into all truth (John 16:13-15).

<u>Family Worship</u>

In preparation for hastily leaving Egyptian captivity, families were commanded to prepare a Passover mean, which would give sustenance for the journey, and also be an occasion of worshipping God through the blood sacrifice of the Lamb. The Passover was established as a family worship ritual celebrated in the home reminding the Jewish people of their deliverance by God from bondage (12:43). Family worship should be the unifying center of the family vs. according to their Father's house; a Father's house here is synonymous "a family."

The Passover is to be the specific family festival of Israel. And it is noteworthy that the first ordinance of the Jewish religion was a domestic service. The Exodus event became the central historical memory. Worship included memory, education and moral commitment. Worship has at least two distinct aspects: adoration or praise, and obedience or service. To worship God is to "serve." Such worship or service is done in reverential fear and wonder of adoring awe, not grudgingly in face of threatened punishment. Service grows out of love and devotion. Worship is not outward actions, as much as inner devotions (Ephesians 5:19; Colossians 3:16). Worship was a family experience. Shared worship is considered so important to the development of faith that believers are warned against neglecting it (Hebrews 10:25).

As in biblical times, families today need to know the word of God by hearing it taught and by worshipping God through family worship in the Church (Deuteronomy 31:12,13). Elkanah and his two wives Hannah and Peninnah were devout in their worship to the Lord, even though Peninnah made fun of Hannah because she had borne no children. Hannah's devotion is clearly set forth in her fervent prayer life, which received God's answer in the birth of Samuel. The depth of her devotion and that of her husband's demonstrated in their willingness to give Samuel to Eli, the Priest, to grow up serving God in the Temple (I Samuel 1:9-28; 2:18-21, 26).

Job's persistent desire was for his children to be acceptable to God. Christian families should continue to offer prayers for God's guidance and forgiveness on behalf of their children (Job 1:5). God established a place of worship for the new nation. The people celebrated their faith through home worship, but on designated holy days, they were to go as households to the Temple and worship joyfully together (Deuteronomy 12:11-14,18; 15:20; 16:11-14). Worship was a family experience shared. Worship is considered so important to the development of faith that believers are warned against neglecting it (Hebrews 10:25). As in biblical times, families today need to know the word of God by hearing it taught and by worshipping God through family worship in the Church (Deuteronomy 12:7).

BIBLIOGRAPHY

King James Version: <u>The Holy Bible</u>. Holman Bible Publisher: Nashville, Tennessee.

Printed in the United States
by Baker & Taylor Publisher Services